FOREVER
IN MY
goodness

FOREVER IN MY goodness

Trusting in the Abundant Favor of God

MORGAN SUGG

LEAFWOOD
PUBLISHERS
an imprint of Abilene Christian University Press

FOREVER IN MY GOODNESS
Trusting in the Abundant Favor of God

LEAFWOOD
PUBLISHERS
an imprint of Abilene Christian University Press

Copyright © 2021 by Morgan Sugg

ISBN 978-1-68426-121-5 | LCCN 2020025770

Printed in the United States of America

ALL RIGHTS RESERVED
No part of this publication may be reproduced, stored in a retrieval system, or transmitted in any form by any means—electronic, mechanical, photocopying, recording, or otherwise—without prior written consent.

Unless otherwise noted, Scripture quotations and summaries are from Tree of Life (TLV) Translation of the Bible. Copyright © 2015 by The Messianic Jewish Family Bible Society.

Scripture quotations noted NKJV are Scripture taken from the New King James Version®. Copyright © 1982 by Thomas Nelson. Used by permission. All rights reserved.

Scripture quotations noted NIV are taken from THE HOLY BIBLE, NEW INTERNATIONAL VERSION®, NIV® Copyright © 1973, 1978, 1984, 2011 by Biblica, Inc.® Used by permission. All rights reserved worldwide.

Scripture quotations noted ESV are taken from The ESV® Bible (The Holy Bible, English Standard Version®). ESV® Text Edition: 2016. Copyright © 2001 by Crossway, a publishing ministry of Good News Publishers. The ESV® text has been reproduced in cooperation with and by permission of Good News Publishers. Unauthorized reproduction of this publication is prohibited. All rights reserved.

Scripture quotations marked TPT are from The Passion Translation®. Copyright © 2017, 2018 by Passion & Fire Ministries, Inc. Used by permission. All rights reserved. ThePassionTranslation.com.

Scripture quotations noted NLT are taken from the Holy Bible, New Living Translation, copyright ©1996, 2004, 2007, 2015 by Tyndale House Foundation. Used by permission of Tyndale House Publishers, Inc., Carol Stream, IL 60188. All rights reserved.

LIBRARY OF CONGRESS CATALOGING-IN-PUBLICATION DATA
Names: Sugg, Morgan, author.
Title: Forever in my goodness : trusting in the abundant favor of God / Morgan Sugg.
Description: Abilene, Texas : Leafwood Publishers, 2021. | Includes bibliographical references.
Identifiers: LCCN 2020025770 (print) | LCCN 2020025771 (ebook) | ISBN 9781684261215 (paperback) | ISBN 9781684269464 (ebook)
Subjects: LCSH: God (Christianity)—Goodness.
Classification: LCC BT137 .S83 2021 (print) | LCC BT137 (ebook) | DDC 231/.8—dc23
LC record available at https://lccn.loc.gov/2020025770
LC ebook record available at https://lccn.loc.gov/2020025771

Cover design by ThinkPen Design | Interior text design by Sandy Armstrong, Strong Design

Leafwood Publishers is an imprint of Abilene Christian University Press
ACU Box 29138
Abilene, Texas 79699

1-877-816-4455 | www.leafwoodpublishers.com

For Brad—

*The way you love me is a true reflection
of your love for Christ.
Thank you for walking with me side by side
and loving me and the boys well.*

Contents

Foreword by Judy Jacobs   9
A Word and Prayer for You   13
Preface: Life Out of Control   15

One—My Goodness Is Honey   19
Two—My Goodness Is Absolute   35
Three—My Goodness Goes Before   51
Four—My Goodness Follows   65
Five—My Goodness Is Guidance   79
Six—My Goodness Brings Repentance   95
Seven—My Goodness Is an Experience   111
Eight—My Goodness Is a Seed   125
Nine—My Goodness Is Working   139
Ten—My Goodness Is a Conversation   153

Epilogue   169
Acknowledgments   171
About the Author   173

Foreword

ONE OF MY FAVORITE PSALMS IS PSALM 23. AS A matter of fact, it was the very first psalm I memorized growing up. My mom and dad were sharecroppers in North Carolina, and I grew up in a culture of church, family, faith, and food, along with my eleven siblings. I loved reading the Bible and memorizing as much as I could. On one particular occasion, I found myself presented with a challenge. My school was offering an opportunity to attend summer camp for free, with the reward going to students who memorized a certain number of chapters and verses from the Bible. I was eager to strike Psalm 23 off my list, because, for me, this would be one of the easiest to get down.

I went through the psalm, declaring Jesus as my good shepherd and, because of that, repeating, "I shall not want." I liked the fact that I could "lay down in green pastures," because as a young girl, I could see myself running through those green pastures with my brother and sister and collapsing in the green blanket of grass, exhausted from running so hard. Oh how sweet would be the smell of the beautiful, freshly cut grass and the blessed feeling of being carefree!

As the psalm continued, I got to the "valley of the shadow of death" line, and I remember thinking, *I want to get through this part of the psalm quickly because it is kind of scary*—and I was also very anxious to get to my favorite part. Then I would lift my head up and put my shoulders back, and with all the confidence in the world, I would continue with, "Surely goodness and mercy shall follow me all the days of my life; and I will dwell in the house of the LORD forever" (NKJV). Whew! There, my favorite part! I loved it!

As a young child, and even into my middle school years and those horrid, awkward teenage years, I never knew how those words—"Surely goodness and mercy shall follow me all the days of my life"—would reverberate over and over in my mind, getting me through some of the most difficult days of my life: getting married; having children; traveling all over the world while raising those children on the road; writing books; ministering before presidents, prime ministers, and dignitaries; being a mentor to hundreds; and now copastoring with my husband of twenty-seven years. The goodness of the Lord ... what would we do without it?

In *Forever in My Goodness*, Morgan Sugg outlines the attributes of this good, good Father. Morgan presents an incredible dissection of the goodness of the Father so we may all see the many-sided goodness of God that we get to enjoy on a daily basis. Her testimony, her clarity of heart, and the rhythm of her beautiful relationship with her God show us the simple joys of knowing him as the intimate Abba Daddy that he is.

If you have ever had to walk the hard road of rejection, bury a child, close a once-successful business, go through a hard divorce, get a pink slip handed to you, or go through other awful life circumstances, then you know how much you have depended upon the goodness and mercy of the Lord. *Goodness* is defined as "moral excellence," "virtue," "kindness," "generosity," or "the best or most valuable part of anything" (I love this), according to *The Free*

Dictionary by Farlex. It even goes on to say *goodness* is "a euphemism for God."

Our God is a good God. I have learned again and again from life lessons that God is indeed good. I believe what Paul says in Romans 8:28: "All things work together for good to those who love God, to those who are the called according to *His* purpose" (NKJV). I have looked at that word *All* every way that I can, and it still remains the same—*all things* means *all things*! Because, "As the heavens are higher than the earth, so are My ways higher than your ways, and My thoughts than your thoughts" (Isa. 55:9 NKJV). I have read the Bible many times, and nowhere does it say, "You shall *understand* the Lord your God." No! It says, "You shall *love* the LORD your God" (Matt. 22:37 NKJV). One thing I have learned is that if I do the loving, he will help me with the understanding.

What dilemma are you facing right now? What tragedy do you find yourself facing at the moment? One thing I love to do is surround myself with people of like-faith, like-destiny, and like-anointing. If I can get around people who have traveled the road before me and can tell me where the bends are in the road, or people who are on the same journey I am and will walk alongside me, then I know my journey is going to be easier. That's what *Forever in My Goodness* is all about. You have an incredible opportunity to travel on a road that Morgan, in many respects, has already traversed; and she leaves us with great markers along the way to get us to the finish line, experiencing the real supernatural goodness of the Lord as we go.

I invite you to take this journey of joy, fulfillment, prosperity, favor, and peace to a place only imaginable if it were not for the goodness of our great God. I promise you, as you read this work, you will forever be living in the abundance and favor of his Goodness!

—Judy Jacobs

A Word and Prayer for You

THE GOOD LIFE IS WHAT WE ALL WANT. WE WERE made to crave a life of goodness, but we often seek goodness as if it were a status instead of seeking Goodness itself. We create an image of what is good in our minds, and when life falls short of the standard we have imagined, we are left with questions. But here is the deal: we don't question ourselves; instead, we doubt God and his goodness. *Why would a good God let this happen?* That question often lingers in the hearts and minds of both believers and nonbelievers.

Life has a way of leaving us searching for goodness. But often, instead of finding real goodness, we force ourselves to believe we see goodness where it doesn't actually exist.

I didn't have a choice in experiencing the gruesome tragedy that fell on a summer day. You didn't have a choice in the abuse that violated your body and mind. You didn't have a choice in the pain you have had to endure. You didn't have a choice in the sickness that has ravaged your body. You didn't have a choice in the death that has ushered in grief.

Life happens, and we often don't get a say in it. But we do get a say in experiencing the goodness of God. Life will shake us, but the goodness of God will sustain us if we know how to find it.

Friend, I want you to know that the goodness of God is more than just an abstract concept we should believe in. It is something we can see, experience, and encounter. My prayer for you is that you see, experience, and encounter the goodness of God like never before. I can assure you that God's goodness is more and does more than we could ever comprehend. But that doesn't mean we have to live blind to the power of goodness. Though we will never fully comprehend God, he longs to show us more and more of his heart. *Forever in My Goodness* will reveal small truths about God's goodness. So, the next time life happens, the goodness of God will not be something you are searching for, but something you are embracing.

God, I ask that as each person reads the words on these pages, you move in their hearts and minds like only you can. Help each person to see that you are the same yesterday, today, and forever. Your goodness has always been and will always be evident in their lives. Holy Spirit, open their eyes to see beyond the pain and into your presence. Reveal your active, never-ending, overflowing goodness in every moment of their lives. In Jesus's name, I pray the enemy is silenced, the lies of the enemy are exposed, and the truth of who you are—your goodness—is revealed. Amen.

Blessings,
Morgan

Preface

Life Out of Control

THE TEARS STREAMING DOWN MY FACE FELT AS warm as the sun beaming in my car while I was driving home from work that day. I was broken. I was broken from living in fear, attempting to cope with anxiety, and pretending like I didn't doubt God. Feeling broken had pushed me to being over it all, and I refused to let the enemy have any more control. So as the tears fell, so did my walls. I finally agreed to ask Jesus where he was the day my world was shaken to its core.

I was scared to ask. I was afraid to enter into this specific conversation. If I asked Jesus where he was that fateful day, I didn't know what I would find. I contemplated asking the simple question as if Jesus didn't know what I wanted to ask. Like the good friend he is, he sat there for two weeks, patiently waiting for me to ask what I am sure he couldn't wait to answer.

This traffic-filled, mundane drive had never been short on conversations. A seventy-mile one-way commute leaves a lot of time for discussion. There wasn't anything that Jesus and I hadn't talked about—well, almost anything. We talked about my marriage, my three boys, work, friends, dreams, purpose, and calling. But there was one area—this one locked-up place in my heart—I hadn't opened up to him. We could chat about anything but that *one* tragic day.

One day while chatting with friends at lunch, no one knowing I had a locked-up moment in my heart, this question was posed: "Do you know where Jesus was in those questionable moments?" After the question was asked at the table, I just thought to myself, *What an interesting question.* But once by myself, I started pondering that thought a bit more. That is when I realized I didn't know where God was on one very important day. That question cracked open the closed door in my heart, leading me to sit quietly in my car.

For two weeks, I sat in a silence that starkly contrasted my normal conversations with God. I knew I needed to ask him where he was that day my faith was shaken, but I didn't know what I would hear. I didn't know what words would lay on the other side of that question.

I wanted to believe I would be content with not knowing where he was that tragic day, but that would require me to be content living with fear and anxiety. That hadn't really been working for me thus far. Fear and anxiety had become the nasty side effects of not knowing the answer to the lingering question. Fear and anxiety drove me into a nasty pit of depression that tempted me to take my own life. Prayer, family, my amazing doctor, and medicine had helped me get back on my feet. Now I sat wondering if it was really necessary to reopen a wound that seemed to be healed.

Though it was now two decades later, inside of me was still a little thirteen-year-old girl standing by the lake, overcome by gruesome tragedy. That girl needed to find Jesus. I was a wife and mother of three by now, but part of me was still stuck. Stuck in a moment that captivated me and blinded me to the goodness of God.

The lake water was refreshing, as my cousins and I splashed and played. The aroma of the warm grill lingered in the air. I helped my two aunts and their girlfriends prepare lunch and played with my cousins as my two uncles and their friends drove off on the Jet Skis for one last ride. Then, in an instant, though the sun still shone, the sky felt gray as the words "There's been an accident" clouded the picturesque day. Less than twenty-four hours earlier, Dale and my uncle Chad had been air boxing as Evander Holyfield and Mike Tyson fought for a title. And now Dale lay dead in the boat, my aunt and uncle grasping for any glimmer of hope, Dale's son in my arms, and his wife beside me—death hovering and goodness missing.

Death has a way of sneaking up on life and snatching it in the most shocking and heart shattering of ways. When this type of chaos starts swirling around us, confusion shows up, often doing a good job of blinding us to the goodness of God. That is what happened to me that day. Every time I let my mind go back to that day, I could see no good; I only saw death win. It seemed God had gone missing for a moment in time, and his goodness had escaped from the tragedy that warped my faith.

Why was I struggling with asking Jesus where he was? It shouldn't be that hard to let him in to that day. God is omnipresent, so he had to be there; his goodness too. But I didn't know where. I had lived that day and hadn't seen him, so why would it be any different when I asked him some twenty years later?

So, Jesus and I sat riding in my car, driving home from work like we had done hundreds of times, when I finally surrendered.

I surrendered the question.

I surrendered my mind.

I surrendered my heart.

I surrendered my doubt.

I surrendered that tragic day.

My mind screamed the question while my lips remained motionless, *WHERE WERE YOU?* The question echoed in the space between the driver's seat and the passenger seat, between heaven and earth.

one

My Goodness Is Honey

As it is impossible to verbally describe the sweetness of honey to one who has never tasted honey, so the goodness of God cannot be clearly communicated by way of teaching if we ourselves are not able to penetrate into the goodness of the Lord by our own experience.

—Saint Basil

HAVE YOU EVER READ CERTAIN BIBLE STORIES AND thought, *That is just plain crazy?* I mean, there are some pretty radical stories in the Bible. A few that come to mind are the crazy plagues that God sent to deliver his people from the Egyptians, when a donkey talked, or the time a sword gets swallowed up in a fat belly (Exod. 7–12; Num. 22; Judg. 3). Stories like these are sure to fill your mind with all kinds of imagery. But one particular character in the Bible lived out many over-the-top stories . . . Samson.

In one story, Samson caught three hundred foxes and tied them together, tail-to-tail, with torches. What? That has got to be at the top of the list for outlandish accounts in the Bible. Then, shortly after that, Samson killed one thousand men with the jawbone of a donkey. Over the top seems ordinary for Samson. So, when Samson encounters a lion, what would seem crazy to us almost appears normal to him (Judg. 15).

Samson had been wandering in the vineyard of Timnah when a young lion attacked him. This lion, like all lions, must have been stalking its prey and found one he thought he could devour. But just as quickly as the lion pounced, so moved the Spirit of the Lord upon Samson. The fight ended as fast as it began. Samson, with his hands that had been built for battle, tore the lion apart. Wild, right? But the story isn't over.

Not too long after his encounter with the lion, Samson was passing by where this battle had taken place, and he turned to look at the carcass of the lion and noticed something unusual. Samson should have stayed away from the dead lion, as he wasn't supposed to come in contact with dead things. But the sight of bees coming from the dead lion was just something to behold. And then Samson saw it, past the bees, in the middle of death: he found sweet honey (Judg. 14).

Moments fill our lives that we were never meant to encounter and choices we shouldn't have made. During our days, we meet moments that are like that dead lion. Moments that change us and often change our perspective of God and his goodness. But if we take time to see past the death, past the swarming bees, we can find amber drops of goodness in the depths of the lion.

Honey

In Texas, honey is a staple in the kitchen. Texans love honey for the same reasons anyone else loves honey. It's good for you, and it tastes sweet. Who wouldn't love that combination? But the real reason any good Texan loves honey is because of the Mexican dessert sopapillas.

Sopapillas are deliciously simple. The deep-fried dough is tossed in a cinnamon and sugar mixture until entirely covered and then served with a side of butter and honey. After drizzling honey on top of the deep-fried goodness, people savor the treat. Honey on a sopapilla is like icing on a cake; it finishes it off, leaving sweet goodness in your mouth with every bite.

While honey is delicious on this dessert, we know that honey is so much more. The slow dripping sweet treat not only reminds us of simpler times but also offers healing for our bodies. My family lives in the rapidly growing town of Frisco, Texas. But even in the booming commerce of the city, you can sense a strong push to keep life somewhat quaint and simple. In the effort to keep this suburban feel, we have a farmer's market. My husband and I love to take our three boys to the market to taste some of the fresh goods brought by farmers. We often buy a fresh-baked loaf of challah bread and then head a few stalls down and buy honey. But we don't just buy any honey. We buy the freshest honey from the most local hive. Why? Because that honey offers us something no other honey can. Local bees pollinate from local flowers to create this goodness. Honey made in the surrounding area provides allergy sufferers access to the liquid gold that helps control the allergies that overtake their sinuses.

More than a delicious addition to a dessert, honey is a wonderful gift from God. The smooth goodness has many benefits —calming a cough, acting as an anti-inflammatory, and healing wounds. Honey is known to have been an everyday treat in Egypt. For centuries, Egyptians have been recognized as beekeepers, using honey to sweeten foods, for medicine, and even for embalming. In the pyramids of Egypt, archeologists have discovered a pot of honey that is still edible. The Egyptians, as well as the Hebrews, knew the power of honey. It brings healing, tastes sweet, and is long-lasting.

The Promise

Honey would have been a delicacy encountered by the Israelites during their grueling days of slavery in Egypt. So why would God call them to a promised land flowing with milk and honey if there had been honey where they had been enslaved? I believe the honey the Israelites would see drip like beautiful gems was a pleasure not offered or at least scarcely offered to them in Egypt. So, when God calls the Israelites to him and gives them a promise of a land "flowing with milk and honey," he promises his children the never-ending flow of his goodness. His goodness that never runs dry, which would bring healing and sweetness and would never spoil.

God spoke words of physical goodness as he painted a picture of the promise in their minds. God wrote his promise of goodness upon the Israelites' hearts. His words, like the sweet nectar, brought refreshment and healing to their enslaved minds.

When we read of the promise of honey, we read of the goodness of God. The goodness of God is as tangible as the ground we walk on and the air we breathe. It is something we can see and trust through experience. Like the Israelites, God has given you the promise of his goodness. His goodness, like honey, is designed to bring sweetness to your life. To enrich your life with a never-ending hope of his presence always with you. His goodness is here to bring you healing. It brings healing to the hurtful, painful, and uncertain moments in our lives. His goodness is a salve that restores our wounds. This liquid gold goodness never fails. Like the three-thousand-year-old pot of honey found in the pyramids of Egypt, the goodness of God is everlasting.[1]

Even to this day, we can still see the faithfulness of God's promise to Israel. Even with the rise and fall of obedience from

God's people, we see that his goodness never stops flowing. To this day, Israel is a top producer of goods and technology for the world, while being one of the smallest countries. We see God's goodness pouring from Israel like honey, supplying products to the world. "Great is your faithfulness. . . . The Lord is good to those whose hope is in him, to the one who seeks him" (Lam. 3:23, 25 NIV).

God is faithful, and his goodness will never fail and will never cease. The goodness of God is the sweet nectar that sustains our lives. God's goodness is far more reaching than we could ever imagine. Because of its eternal nature, it presses beyond our mortal comprehension and draws us closer to him.

What Is Goodness?

How do you define "goodness"? How do you determine what is good and what is not? Your definition of goodness is probably very different from mine. So, let's get technical for just a brief moment. Dictionary.com defines "goodness" as "the state or quality of being good; moral excellence; virtue; kindly feeling; kindness; generosity." Here's the deal: we can read the definition of "goodness" all we want, but the reality is that we all have our own personal standard or measurement of what good is. Each of us—based on personal experience, our preference, our interpretation of the things around us—creates a worldview. That worldview becomes the lens through which we filter everything we come in contact with, determining if it is good or not.

I am a good person, and I bet you are too. According to the definition above, most of us are "good." But we all too often decide who is good and what is good based on our personal filters.

We do something because it feels good.

We eat something because it smells or looks good.

We buy something because it's a good deal.

We are friends with someone because she is good.

We often make decisions and judgments of what is good or not by holding up our human-made measuring stick. This self-created filter often distorts our definition and understanding of goodness. So when something does not turn out as we had expected, we blame and question God. As Ron Brackin notes, "the words 'good' and 'love' have become so trivialized in our culture—not that our definitions were so accurate to begin with—that, in times of distress or disappointment, we struggle to believe that God is either."[2]

We struggle with God's goodness because we are trying to understand it through the wrong lens. Harsh truth moment: it doesn't matter if we think we are good and things around us are good, because life will happen, and when life shakes us, our version of "good" will come crumbling down around us. We will be left standing in a heap of our worldview, wondering where God was and how a good God would let life happen like this.

When we have a skewed understanding of the goodness of God, then we will often live in a cyclical pattern of highs and lows, never entirely breaking free from unnecessary struggle. God desires for us to live a life of complete freedom that is full of purpose. But if we do not have a correct view of God's goodness, we will always live less than God has intended.

Our skewed and misguided understanding of goodness causes us to have an unrecognized, thin layer of doubt, or even a gaping chasm of doubt—both of which we try to deny. If we want to understand the real goodness of God, a basic definition will not suffice. We have to lay down our human-made measuring guide. We have to allow the Holy Spirit to help us take off our stained lenses and see through his eyes. Our vision becomes layered with the distortions of this world, and if we don't take time to allow the Holy Spirit to correct our vision, we never see clearly. We must be willing to let our hearts and minds see real goodness from our Creator.

The Enemy

The goodness of God was meant to enhance our lives. But the enemy wants to do nothing but distort who God is, causing us to live less than free lives. We have a very real enemy that is doing everything he can to weaken our faith. He is waiting for moments when we are distracted or caught off guard to pounce and speak a lie of doubt about who God is. There aren't any new tricks in the enemy's playbook. He only has the lie he believed that caused him to fall. He believed he could be higher than God. That lie sent him in a tailspin, and that was all he was left with. With only a lie in his pocket, the devil tries to use it to prey on us. We have seen it in play since the beginning of time. Satan proposed a lie about who God was to Eve and Adam too. "Did God really say, 'You must not eat from all the trees of the garden'?" (Gen. 3:1).

All he did was wait for a moment and seized it, casting questions on who God is. The same is true in our lives. He is waiting for a moment. It can be a moment of pain, hurt, or grief. It could be a moment of joy and surprise. It could be a moment of vulnerability. We must always be on guard, ready to ward off the lie. The lie is the same; it never changes—the words may change, but the intent never does. The intention is to cause you to doubt whom God is. Satan knows he cannot pluck you from the hand of God. But he will do everything in his power to trick you into giving up and giving in. God desires for you to walk in his goodness. And if we want to walk freely in our purpose, we need to understand the goodness of God. We must realize goodness is not a thing; it is who God is. He is goodness.

Goodness Is Not a Thing

Have you ever sat in church and said the *God is good* mantra? You know, when the preacher says into the microphone, "God is good all the time!" Then he extends the mic out to the audience as they chant back, "And all the time, God is good!" I have sat in more church services than I can count where the audience repeats this icebreaker as a preacher enters the pulpit. I, like any good church-goer, say the words as the preacher instructs. Here is the truth: I have flippantly said this phrase too many times. I have repeated it because the preacher told us to—not because I fully believed it.

Who wants to actually admit they aren't sure God is good all the time? What kind of Christian would I be! I have learned saying God is good is very different than seeing and experiencing his goodness. I lived too many years saying God was good but feeling, in my heart, as if his goodness had abandoned me. If we are going to understand goodness, then we have to move from just saying God is good, take off our lenses, and see goodness through Scripture. God desires for us to know his heart, and his heart is good. God wants his goodness revealed in every moment of our lives and for us to know that goodness is not something God does; it is something he is.

God does not have to try to be good. We, on the other hand, have to put forth an effort to extend goodness. We make a conscious decision to be good and do good. As my husband, Brad, and I raise our three boys, we are continually training and teaching them. We have to show them what is good and what is wrong. They have to decide to do good or bad. As image-bearers, goodness is planted deep in us when God forms us in the womb. But that trait must be cultivated. God, on the other hand, does not have to decide to be good. He is good all the time. It is his character, and it cannot change. God is "merciful and gracious, longsuffering, and abounding in goodness and truth, keeping mercy for thousands, forgiving iniquity and transgression and sin" (Exod. 34:6–7 NKJV).

God abounds in goodness. Goodness is an overflowing part of God's character, just like love. God does not and cannot turn off his love for his children. The same is true with his goodness. God's goodness cannot be turned on and off. It is a current that never ceases and a constant steady flow like honey dripping from a comb.

One of my favorite holidays is *Thanksmas Eve*. Yes, it's a made-up combination of holidays. It is the period from the first of November to New Year's Eve. I could list all the reasons these two months are my favorite, but I'll spare you the long list and give you two reasons: family and food! My family is great, but I want to get to the food—the pumpkin pie. Pumpkin pie is my absolute favorite pie—it is creamy, with a beautiful blend of spices and a crust that is golden and flaky, topped with a cloud of whipped cream. A slice of pumpkin pie is pure deliciousness in my mouth. But that is just what it is: a slice of the pie. Before I go back for seconds—who am I kidding, maybe even thirds—I wait to see if others will want pie too. There is only so much pie to go around. But the character of God, who he is, is not like that pie at the holidays. There isn't a limited amount of himself that he rations off to his children.

God isn't just sitting high above us, portioning out his goodness. His goodness is a part of who he is, not something he just hands out. God does not sit high above us, judging us on how good we have been and then deciding how much of him we deserve. He doesn't say, "She acted sinful today; I am only going to give her a small sliver of goodness," and then to another say, "I really like that guy; I am going to give him a huge piece with extra whipped cream." No, God is more than that. He is more than a father who distributes himself. God is the very essence of good. Goodness is a property of who he is. He does not allocate his goodness; his goodness exists in everything he has done, is doing, and will do.

People make bad choices, but God does not. God does not choose to be good or bad, to do good or bad; he is good. His goodness is all around; it never leaves nor forsakes, because he never leaves nor forsakes us. If the goodness of God ceased even for a moment, the entire universe would vanish. We would cease to exist, because he has breathed goodness into everything he created. God, in his eternal goodness, gave his everything for us to open our eyes and to restore our lives.

Forrest of Goodness

In 1 Samuel 14, we read that King Saul, who is quite the character, placed his men under oath, saying they could not eat any food until he had avenged his enemies. He didn't care about his men becoming hungry and angry. Now, as the Israelites entered the forest, honey lay on the ground. That honey was a promise to them from God, which their king is now withholding from them. Jonathan, Saul's son, returned from fighting and did not know about the oath when he joined the ranks in the forest.

> But Jonathan had not heard when his father made the people swear the oath. So he put out the end of the staff that was in his hand and dipped it into the honeycomb, put his hand to his mouth—and his eyes brightened. Then, one of the soldiers told him, "Your father strictly put the people under oath saying: 'Cursed be the man that eats food today.' But the troops are exhausted."
>
> Jonathan said, "My father has troubled the people. Just look how my eyes have brightened because I tasted a little of this honey." (1 Sam. 14:27–29)

Jonathan had been out battling and needed nourishment. When he joined the ranks in the forest, he noticed the promise given to his forefathers: honey on the ground. Jonathan reached with his staff and ate the sweetness, and as soon as he tasted it, his eyes brightened. The goodness of God has a way of illuminating our lives. It brings light in dark places and makes the best moments so much sweeter. The goodness of God revives a tired soul and brings hope to the weary heart.

Saul, concerned only with his own pride and not the well-being of his people, made a rash decision. If Saul had been the leader he was initially called to be, he would have recognized the honey in the forest. He would have known the goodness of God before him. We will face people, situations, ourselves, and an enemy that will distract us from the goodness of God. We must be willing to see honey on the ground of the forest and in the depths of the lion, reach down, pick it up, and taste it. The goodness of God is in the most obvious of places, and in it the most unlikely of moments. The goodness of God brightens our eyes, renews our strength, and brings healing to our lives.

Eat the Honey

If we are really going to understand God's goodness, we need to dive deep into the Word that brings hope, life, and healing. We need to see how the goodness of God, woven in the Scriptures, creates a beautiful masterpiece. Then we can see the wonderful thread of goodness streaming through our own lives. Sometimes we have to eat the honey to see the goodness.

> Then He said to me, "Son of man, eat what you find—eat this scroll. Then go, speak to the house of Israel." So I opened my mouth, and He gave me that scroll to eat, as He said to me, "Son of man, feed your belly with this scroll that I am giving you and fill your stomach with it." I ate it and it tasted sweet as honey. (Ezek. 3:1–3)

Ezekiel and God are having a moment. God revealed eternal concepts to an earthly man. Ezekiel, being a man of God, submitted his heart and mind to see the extravagant revelations God had in store. These revelations would not only confirm our Savior but would also draw people to him until his return. If we want to fix our focus on what the real goodness of God looks like, we have to, like Ezekiel, submit our hearts and minds. When we do, God will reveal the truth of his eternal goodness. God can do that in dreams and vision as he did with Ezekiel, and we will get to that in a few chapters. But it is important to recognize that Ezekiel ate the scroll. And the scroll tasted as sweet as honey. We must be consumers of the Word, allowing its sweetness to expose the eternal truths of the goodness of God.

John the Baptist, who is often compared to Ezekiel, had a special diet—one that I I think most of us would not prefer. He ate locusts and honey—crunchy and smooth. Honey does make my sopapilla taste good, but does it make locusts taste good too? I know a lot of people who have switched their diets to various biblical standards and fasts. But I don't know a single person who has ever participated in the *John the Baptist Diet.* Have you ever wondered why he had this special diet? Then wondered why there was a need to make sure we all knew about the special menu? Questions like that run through my mind as I read Scripture. Strange diet? Absolutely. Important? You bet!

John's two-part diet seems simple enough, but how many of you know that simple with God is extravagant? Part one of John's diet: locusts. Locusts were not a household staple in the Bible. They are consumers; they are to do the eating, not be eaten. So, John, in his humble lifestyle, consumed the consumers. Part two of the diet: honey. John enjoyed eating the sweetness of the land. He was eating the never-ending promise. Like Ezekiel and John, we must eat the all-consuming Word of God so that it begins to envelop every part of our lives. When we do, we are partaking in the everlasting promise that is like sweet honey in our mouths. If we want to grasp the goodness of God, we have to consume his Word and let the sweet taste overwhelm our lives, bringing the revelation of the eternal truth of his goodness to our earthly hearts and minds. When we do this, we will begin to see the goodness of God all around us.

Find the Honey

Charles Spurgeon said, "By the help of the divine Spirit . . . we may find honey in the lion."[3] The goodness of God is finding honey in the lion that tried to destroy us. The goodness of God is in the battle we face with the lion. The goodness of God is in the very bees that make the honey. The goodness of God is the Spirit that awakens us when we have been focusing on the wrong thing. The goodness of God is in the liquid gold deep in the lion, waiting for us to see, taste, and offer to the world around us the amber drops of grace. The goodness of God is all around us, waiting for us to feast on it so that we can offer the same sweet truth to a world in need. Like Samson, God calls us to provide the heavenly goodness to those we meet. But we cannot offer something we have not picked up and embraced. Spurgeon continues:

> We have such a living swarm of bees to make honey for us in the precious promises of God, that there is more delight in store than any of us can possibly realise. There is infinitely more of Christ beyond our comprehension than we have as yet been able to comprehend. How blessed to receive of his fulness, to be sweetened with his sweetness, and yet to know that infinite goodness still remains.[4]

There is infinite goodness infused in our lives through the life, death, and resurrection of Jesus Christ. There is a steady current of goodness flowing through us by the power of the Holy Spirit, revealing goodness in every mountain we climb and every valley we cross. The goodness of God is everywhere we go, in every moment of our lives, because God is good. His goodness never ceases. His goodness was, is, and is to come.

If we want to grasp this goodness, we have to do more than believe he is good—we need to see it; we need to experience it; we need to taste it like honey drizzled over our lives. The sweetness of honey is attractive, but its allure is much deeper than being sweet. Likewise, the goodness of God is something sweet, but it is also so much more profound. Sometimes we have to reach into the deep of a dead lion to find it, and other times it dances among us in the air we breathe.

As I went on a search for goodness, I found that God's goodness is more than a state or something that happens. It is living and breathing. It moves with you and me. We can see it, taste it, experience it, live it, give it, and pray it. Excavating deep in the soil of God's Word, the Holy Spirit uncovered gems of goodness that brought healing, sweetness, grace, and that breathed life into my soul. God's goodness is so much more than just good; it is great.

As you read the following pages, let the honey drip over your life, revealing the promise of his great goodness.

Chapter One Reflection

1. Take a moment to evaluate your personal definition of "good."

2. Does your definition of "good" line up with your worldview or with God's character?

3. Before we move forward, take a prayerful moment and allow the Holy Spirit to show you if there is a moment when you have questioned or doubted the goodness of God.

Notes

[1] Natasha Geiling, "The Science Behind Honey's Eternal Shelf Life," Smithsonian Institution, August 22, 2013, https://www.smithsonianmag.com/science-nature/the-science-behind-honeys-eternal-shelf-life-1218690/.

[2] "A Quote by Ron Brackin," Goodreads, accessed June 12, 2019, https://www.goodreads.com/quotes/1236806-the-words-good-and-love-have-become-so-trivialized-in.

[3] C. H. Spurgeon, "Hands Full of Honey," in *The Metropolitan Tabernacle Pulpit Sermons*, vol. 29 (London: Passmore & Alabaster, 1883), 61.

[4] Spurgeon, "Hands Full of Honey," 61.

two

My Goodness Is Absolute

There is no creature so small and abject, that it representeth not the goodness of God.

—Thomas à Kempis

- God spoke light into existence, separating the day and night, making evening and night . . . it was good.
- God spoke for the sky to appear, separating the waters above and below, and the ground appeared . . . it was good.
- God spoke for soft grass, green plants, and fruit trees to sprout . . . it was good.
- God spoke for the sun to rule the day, and the moon and stars to oversee the night, setting in place signs and seasons, days and years . . . it was good.
- God spoke, and creatures swarmed the seas, and others filled the sky . . . it was good.
- God spoke, and wild animals, along with crawling creatures and livestock, began to wander on the dry ground . . . it was good.
- God spoke and blessed the man and woman he created in their image . . . it was very good.

As God created this wondrous world, he finished each creation off with goodness. He called every day and everything good (Gen. 1). Like a king sealing a decree, God sealed his handiwork with his goodness. His goodness holds the world together:

- It holds the waters in place.
- It keeps the land exposed.
- It causes the flowers to bloom.
- It allows the trees to stand.
- It reveals prophecy.
- It shines in the day and glows in the night.
- It is in every breath we breathe.

God's goodness never ceases to exist; the sustainability of the world relies on it. The goodness of God is the very bedrock of truth for our faith. When he laid the foundation of our world, he sealed it with his goodness. The goodness of God is the truth; it is never-ending; it is absolute.

What Is Absolute?

We use the words "absolute" or "absolutely" to add emphasis to what we are trying to communicate: "I had the absolute best time!" "That was absolutely the best thing I have ever tasted!" "There is absolutely no way I am doing that!" We use this word among thousands of others to articulate what we are feeling without truly understanding their deeper or real meaning. I'm guilty! I once heard someone say this same thing about the word "awesome." We use awesome flippantly when nothing is truly awesome but God. I still use the word "awesome," and I still use the word "absolute." But often, as they slip out of my mouth, I catch myself and ask a simple question: Was there a more accurate word I could have used? Sometimes I come up with one, but other times, not so much.

I am not saying we can't use the word "absolute" in our emphatic descriptions of life, but I do think we need to understand its real definition. We can't let our extreme use of a word dilute the true meaning of it. Understanding "absolute" will help us see the only real absolute is Jesus, our goodness.

Let's get technical just for a brief moment. "Absolute," like most words, carries the weight of many definitions; this gives the word different meaning in different contexts or various situations. According to *Merriam-Webster Dictionary*, "absolute" can mean the following:

> free from imperfection; perfect
> free or relatively free from mixture; pure
> having no restriction, exception, or qualification
> positive, unquestionable
> independent of arbitrary standards of measurement

These are just a few of the many definitions and descriptions of "absolute." We often use this word in our vocabulary when it suits us but are quick to reject it when it confines us.

There is a sushi restaurant that has my favorite sushi roll: Lady Karen. It is crabmeat and asparagus rolled in cucumber strips instead of rice. If you and I were having a conversation about sushi, it is very likely I would tell you about this particular roll. It is also very likely I would use a phrase like this: "My favorite sushi roll is called Lady Karen; is it absolutely the best!" There it is—that word, describing my favorite rolled-up seafood.

Lady Karen is my favorite sushi roll and is the absolute best— the absolute best in *my* world. In reality, it is probably far from the absolute best. I haven't tried all the sushi this world has to offer, leaving the Lady Karen the absolute best in my small world but far from the absolute best. Here I am using this strong word for what I believe is the absolute best sushi roll. I have taken the word and made it fit into the context in which I want it to fit. While I don't believe there is anything wrong with using the word to describe one of my favorite foods, I must be careful not to assume all my absolutes are truth.

You Do You

"Friend, you do you!"

"You do you, and I'm gonna do me."

"This is my truth."

"Speak your truth."

I have heard sayings like these and read memes with those phrases more times than I could count. It's not farfetched for "you do you" to be said while at lunch with some girlfriends. I have some of the best girlfriends one could hope for, but just like all women, we go through phases of eating healthy. Unfortunately, not all of us ever happen to be "eating healthy" at the same time, and I'm never the one eating "clean." So, a couple of girls might order something really clean and healthy, while others order all the carbs the menu has to offer. Me, I order all the carbs—the white ones, the really bad ones—and a Dr. Pepper, too. At that moment, one of us, I mean me, might say, "Sorry . . . I am so hungry; I need bread!" and then others will jokingly reply, "You do you!" Everyone laughs and continues with lunch.

Phrases like this, I think, are meant to be a form of encouragement to be yourself and stand up for what you believe to be right, to eat the carbs. But there has been a shift that has taken place. We have moved from encouragement to narcissism. The trend in society right now is you do what is right for you, and I will do what is right for me. You speak your truth, and I will speak my truth. Because truth is relative, right? Wrong!

Let me stop right there and say it as plainly as I can that that is a lie from the pit of hell. "Your truth is relative to you, and mine is relative to me" is a twisted lie the enemy has spread through the earth. And we have accepted the lie because we don't want to stir the pot. We should be for encouraging each other and lifting one another up because, yes, we were all made to live out a God-given purpose uniquely tailored for each of us. But I'm not going to encourage you to live a life that seems absolutely true to you but directly opposes our Absolute Goodness.

You want to have your truth, and you want me to have mine, but when life gets turned upside down and everything falls apart, we don't want the responsibility of our own life sucking. There is a heavy price to pay for *your own truth*, for *you doing you* without regard to what God says, for creating your own absolutes. We want our own absolutes, our own standards for life, but then we want to blame God for not being good. God is the only truth, the only absolute. When we let go of our truth, of our human-made absolutes, and lean into his, then we see his Absolute Goodness.

The world we live in would like us to believe there are no absolutes. Because if there were absolutes, that would make things in this life black and white. No one wants to live life with a line drawn in the sand, right? So, if we live in a world where nothing is right or wrong, then everyone is free.

Free to live as they wish.

Free to talk as they wish.

Free to love as they wish.

Free to do what they wish.

A life of no absolutes gives me the absolute freedom to live however I deem good for me. But it seems in our selfish ambition, we created our own absolute. This idea stems from a concept called *moral relativism*. Relativism is the idea that truth and morality exist in relation to society and culture and are not absolute.[1] But the very fact that I say there are no absolutes means I am, in fact, creating an absolute. Absolutes are inevitable. You cannot logically argue there are no absolutes. That in itself is contradictory.

What if this concept of absolutes isn't one we are supposed to reject or argue? Maybe absolutes are something we were meant to embrace. Absolute Goodness was revealed at creation, exposing the life of freedom we were meant to live. We all crave a life of freedom, and God has offered that to you and me, yet we still seem to take on our own personal truth. To understand the goodness of God, we must understand absolutes. We must settle in our hearts and fix our minds on the fact that there is only one absolute truth, only one Absolute Goodness.

Earthly Absolute

My dad taught me a lesson on this subject when I was a young girl. As a youth pastor, he taught all the young people he came in contact with this same lesson. My dad, in a very wise and practical way, would say, "I can guarantee you, if you never drink a drop of alcohol, you will never become an alcoholic," and, "I can guarantee you, if you never do drugs, you will never become an addict." These statements are logical and almost bring a sense of simplicity to the actions. My dad was right. We have a choice to believe in the simplicity of absolutes.

We all create our own earthly absolutes that are absolutely true to us. But that does not make them actually true or even absolute. We could sit for hours and discuss the absolutes of our lives. There are books and books written by philosophers that argue the validity versus the irrationality of absolutes, each believing they are absolutely right.

There is a simplicity in believing in absolutes as my father taught me. But there is pride in believing that my absolutes are the right ones—each of us surrounding ourselves with our personal absolutes that are really just opinions. There is no human-made absolute that can withstand eternity. The Goodness of God is a bedrock truth of Scripture.[2] God is good, and because he is good, he does good, and this will absolutely never change.

When we build our faith with our own personal absolutes, we are like the man we read about in Matthew who built his house on sand. When the storm arrived, the winds blew, and the water rose, his house came crashing down (Matt. 7:24–27). But if we build our life on the absolute truth and goodness of the Word, of Scripture, we will experience goodness that never fails. We must build our lives on the bedrock of the only absolute truth: Jesus. Then when the storms come, the waters rise, and winds blow, we will be left standing in awe of God, because we trusted in his Absolute Goodness. Jesus never said to anyone, "You do you!" He didn't say, "I am the way, the truth, and the life," in order for you to create your own truth (John 14:6).

Matthew 19 tells the story of the rich young ruler who asks Jesus, "Teacher, what good shall I do to have eternal life?" (Matt. 19:16). It is essential to see how Jesus responds to the rich young ruler, but it is equally important to note how Jesus does not respond. Jesus does not counter with "Live your truth, bro. You do you! Be good, and you will absolutely have eternal life." Jesus does not respond by saying, "You do what feels good to you, be true to yourself, and this will give you eternal life." Jesus responds in love with the only absolute truth of Scripture. What Jesus actually says is, "Why do you ask Me about what is good? . . . There is only One who is good; but if you want to enter into life, keep the commandments" (Matt. 19:17). We can live our truth and pretend there are no absolutes, building our world on the sand, creating our own absolute that will come crashing down. Or we can align our hearts and minds with the only Truth, the only one who is Absolutely good who can guarantee an absolute eternal life.

FOREVER IN MY *goodness*

Goodness Is Absolute

We live in a world of created absolutes. We create them, or other people create them for us. Our minds are flooded with man-made absolutes, especially when it comes to health diagnoses. I need you to know I love doctors. I am grateful for doctors and believe they are essential for our health. My family has been blessed to have been treated by some of the best physicians. I have a cousin who is a physician's assistant, and he is one of the best you could ever find. But doctors are trained to speak the facts they see, and sometimes those facts seem to present earthly absolutes. But there is only one absolute: God in his goodness is absolute.

Detra

One day, I received a phone call from my mom. It's one of those calls where when you answer the phone, you know instantly something is not right. My mom began to tell me that a cousin of mine who lived in Midland, Texas, had suffered a stroke, and it did not look hopeful. My entire family began to pray as we awaited more information to come in from the doctors. Living in Frisco, some five hours from Midland, my mom and I got in the car and drove to be with our family and help in any way we could. The doctors would reveal that Detra had a tumor that had surrounded her heart, causing a stroke. The stroke had fired to all four quadrants of her brain, causing severe damage.

Detra lay on the bed in ICU, tubes everywhere, all in an attempt to keep her alive. The doctors told our family there was no way she would recover from this. There was no way they could do surgery on her heart to remove the tumor. The tumor would continue to cause strokes, and she would die. They wanted to move her to hospice so that she could die in peace, surrounded by family. The doctors said there was absolutely no way she would recover, and there was absolutely nothing they could do to help her. We all have or know someone who has received this grim news: *I am sorry. There is nothing we can do.* Those words are a shot to the heart and our hope. But in the midst of those earthly absolutes that want to cloud our faith, we go to prayer and stand on the hope of our goodness—that his absolute will win.

So, the doctors were right—sort of. There was absolutely nothing they could do, but when God is involved, there is no earthly absolute that overrides his Absolute Goodness. God did absolutely revive her body. God did absolutely dissolve the tumor that had intertwined itself around her heart. God did absolutely reverse the damage to her brain. God's goodness is absolute.

Brandon

My parents and I had been in Tennessee for a quick trip; my dad had just received his pastoral ordination. We were traveling home, which at the time was in Midland, Texas. We had fourteen hours of travel behind us and only four to go, and then we would be home sweet home. Then the cell phone rang. My mom, who was in the passenger seat, answered it. It was Ann, the mom of my brother Brandon's best friend. She spoke one sentence: "There has been an accident, and I don't know if Brandon is okay."

My mom did not say a word in reply but instead calmly extended the phone from the passenger seat to my dad in the driver seat. She reached down and grabbed her Bible out of her purse, pressed it against her chest, and began to pray. She did not stop praying for four hours. My dad stayed on the phone for a few minutes and then hung up. He set the cruise control at seventy miles per hour, gripped the steering wheel at ten and two, and drove calmly for four more hours.

My brother had been in a horrible car wreck, and at the time of that initial phone call, we did not know if he was alive. Later, we received the news that he was alive, but we did not know the extent of his injuries. Four hours later, we arrived at the hospital to find my brother awake and talking, but with bad news from the doctor. He had broken his first, third, and fourth vertebrae.

Technical moment: typically, you can survive broken third and fourth vertebrae, but the first vertebra . . . he should have already been dead or at the very least paralyzed. But he wasn't. The doctors were at a loss. They were grateful he was alive and not paralyzed, but there was nothing they could do for him; surgery on the first vertebra was too dangerous. There it is again—nothing they could do. They couldn't do surgery. They could only stabilize his neck, which was dangerous enough. A couple of days later, they did another scan of his neck and found that the first vertebra was no longer broken. It was completely whole. Surgery on the rest of the neck was now an option.

The doctors were at a loss; there was absolutely nothing they could do. But once again, earthly absolutes do not stand a chance to the only one who is absolute. God absolutely healed that first vertebra. God used the doctors to restore the third and fourth vertebrae. God absolutely brought my brother back. God's Absolute Goodness overrides any absolute this world fires our way.

Sarah and Elizabeth

In the book of Genesis, we read of Sarah and Abraham, who were unable to conceive a child. Sarah was old, and she was barren. There was earthly absolute staring into her aging eyes every day. Now, let's move to the New Testament, to the book of Luke. Remember, Luke was a physician and wrote the only Gospel to record the story of Zechariah and Elizabeth. Elizabeth, like her sister Sarah, many years before her, was barren and old. Again, an earthly absolute was staring her in the face.

God wove his goodness into the very fact that he chose Luke to write about the barren Elizabeth. Luke, the physician, would have known there was no way Elizabeth could have a baby. Sarah and Elizabeth were hundredss of years apart yet joined by the barrenness of their womb—sisters in the club of *I am sorry; you will never have a baby. There is nothing we can do.*

But once again, the Absolute Goodness of God overrides the earthly absolutes that want to keep us bound together and hold us back. The Absolute Goodness of God opened both Sarah's and Elizabeth's wombs. Against all the odds. Against the physicians' absolutes. The goodness of God is absolutely more powerful than the absolute barrenness of this world. Husbands and wives, keep pressing on. You don't have to accept barrenness; instead, keep up the hope of knowing God will deliver his goodness to you. Keep praying and draw close to one another; but more importantly, continue leaning into God—his Absolute Goodness will prevail.

Ties That Bind

We receive earthly absolute reports that shake us to our core and feel like a punch in the stomach. Maybe it is someone else who spoke the absolute. Or perhaps you spoke it yourself:

- I will never love you again.
- My marriage will never survive.
- You will never amount to anything.
- I will never be free from addiction.
- You will always be a failure.
- I will never be forgiven.
- You will never have a baby.
- I will never be loveable.

These are only a few examples of absolutes that we might speak about ourselves, or that others may have spoken about you. We accept these words as absolute truths for our lives, and they become ties that bind us. They become the strongholds that hold us back from trusting in the Absolute Goodness of God and trick us into believing that our own absolute truth is better. We find ourselves bound in a pit of our absolutes. But the Son of our God in heaven died on the cross for you and me, was raised to life for you and me, and won the battle of absolutes for you and me. He is the only absolute. And only a good God has the absolute victory.

Absolute of Absolutes

Lastly, we see our Absolute do the most absolute miracle of all, the miracle that would settle any discussion of goodness or any debate of authority: Jesus came to earth to proclaim the Good News to the poor, set the captives free, heal the blind, free the oppressed, and proclaim the year of the Lord (Luke 4:18–19). In line with this purpose, we read of his many acts of grace, discipline, love, and forgiveness. We can read of the times Jesus raised people from the dead—specifically Lazarus. While Jesus had raised others, Lazarus had been dead for four days. No one had ever been brought to life after this length of time. But Jesus, in his Absolute Goodness, raised his friend and performed a miracle that blew every absolute the people had ever known out of the water. But Jesus was just getting started (John 11).

Jesus would take our place on the cross. He would die for our sins and sickness. He would take our place so that we could live in hope. But the one who had been raising others from the dead was now the one who was dead. The one who died demonstrating absolute goodness would soon be raised back up as our Absolute Goodness.

Jesus died by crucifixion, which was reserved for the worst of the worst. He was accused, beaten, forced to carry his cross, nailed to the cross, and lifted high for all to see. And with his last breath, Jesus uttered, "It is finished" (John 19:30). I don't know of any other words that are more absolute than those he said with his last breath. The rejoicing accusers and the grieving followers received the finality of what had just taken place. The Savior of the world uttered the most absolute words one could say and died. The earth began to shake, and darkness set in. Jesus's followers' worlds were being rocked both emotionally and physically, while I'm sure they were feeling as if goodness were slipping away. As darkness overtook the earth, it must have felt like all the life God had spoken was being undone. Their entire world, our whole world, was being destroyed.

This world will offer absolutes, though they want you to believe there are none. It may even seem as if our faith is dying and covered in darkness. It may have looked as if "it is finished" meant the end. But "it is finished" was just the beginning. They didn't see it the way it was intended for them to view it. It may look like your world as you know it is finished. It may seem like the goodness of God has been overcome by this world. But when Jesus uttered those final words, he sealed the deal that he is the only absolute in this world. He is our eternal life, our Absolute Goodness. You can rest assured that if you feel as if there is no solid ground to stand on, that darkness and death have won, Jesus has already declared it is finished. He is our firm foundation; he is our Absolute Goodness.

The goodness of God is our absolute in this life. We will encounter absolutes of this world that will leave us empty, hurt, or lost. People, test results, words, and jobs will all hurl absolutes our direction. These absolutes will try to weaken our faith. They will try to ignite doubt of God's goodness. While we may not always receive the answers the way we want, that does not diminish God's goodness. The goodness of God will always prevail. There is one absolute in this life: He died on the cross. He was raised back up. He is seated on the throne, continually making intercession for you and me. Jesus Christ is our Absolute Goodness. Absolute Goodness is in every moment; it never leaves; it never forsakes.

While God is good, he is more than some abstract concept of goodness, or goodness discussed in a difficult exegetical conversation. His goodness is personal, and it can be seen best in his actions with people. But we must lay down our truths and our human-made absolutes that distort the goodness of God in our minds. He sent Jesus to demonstrate his goodness to his people. Now his goodness is flowing through the power of the Holy Spirit to every part of our lives. But we will miss God's goodness if we don't surrender our truth at the cross and embrace our personal Absolute Goodness—the only absolute good that exists.

Chapter Two Reflection

1. Have you created personal absolutes that have become foundational truths that don't align with God's Word? If so, take a minute to let go of those ideas and replace them with the truth of God's Word.

2. What earthly absolutes have you received (e.g., doctors' reports, financial statements, relationship status)? Take a moment and write those down. Then search Scripture for what God says to be true. Write those Scriptures down and pray them over those earthly absolutes.

Notes

[1] "Moral Relativism," Moral Relativism, accessed August 17, 2019, https://www.moral-relativism.com/.

[2] Carl B. Bridges Jr., "Good, Goodness," in *Evangelical Dictionary of Biblical Theology*, electronic ed., Baker Reference Library (Grand Rapids: Baker Book House, 1996), 305.

three

My Goodness Goes Before

You go before Him with the blessings of goodness.
—Charles Spurgeon

Have you ever asked for one thing only to receive something different? Or received what you asked for, just not in the way you thought you would? This has happened to all of us. This happens with my boys all the time. Especially as we head into that favorite season of mine—*Thanksmas Eve*. My boys, like most kids, ask for something when we go to the store. Harrison, our youngest, asks almost every day if it's "toy day" in the hopes that I will take him to the store for a toy. I love to buy my boys something special when I can, even when it's something small. But as we head into the holiday season, I know they will receive many gifts from Brad and me and our families.

Often during this time, when they ask to buy a "prize" as they call it, the answer is no. I often get eyes of disappointment from the older two and eyes puddled with tears from the youngest. But a lot of times, what they don't know is that Brad and I have already scouted out what we think they would like for Christmas. More than that, there are many times when they pick something up off a shelf or a rack to ask for it, and Brad and I have already bought that very thing and have hidden it in our house, or maybe it's sitting in our Amazon cart. Long before they started thinking about gifts, Brad and I went before them and started looking for what they would like, for what gifts would excite their hearts and faces. Long before the boys knew it, we went ahead of them and started preparing a way for them. Our Father in heaven does the same thing, but oh so much better. The goodness of God goes before us, preparing a way, forging a path, for us to experience the glory of God.

Paved Goodness

One morning, I left my house for my almost-daily run—headphones in my ears, rocking out to a little Tasha Cobbs Leonard. I typically run the same route every day. I know the course, I know the distance, and I know the pace to keep. I like what is familiar. But on this day, the familiarity caused boredom, and I was getting weary. That is when I noticed a cement path to my right and took it. I darted off my typical path onto a track I didn't know. I didn't know where this path would lead. I didn't know how I would get back home. I didn't know how long it would take me. I was in uncharted territory—for me anyway. And that is when the Lord started speaking.

The path I was now running on, though it was unfamiliar and new to me, had been planned out and paved by someone long before I ever took that route. I didn't know exactly where the path would lead, but the person who had gone before me and paved it did. So, I kept running in peace. Just like the creator of that simple pathway had gone before me, so does the goodness of God. God's goodness goes before us, making a way. We may not know where it is going to lead or when we are going to get there, but we can rest assured that because goodness has gone before, we can experience his glory at the end.

That is precisely what the goodness of God does; it goes before us every day of our lives. The goodness of God goes before us, preparing the way for us to experience the good gifts he has for us. God's goodness is not an afterthought that swoops down in an attempt to fix something that has gone wrong. God does not sit and watch our world come crumbling down and then think he better send in the clean-up team. His goodness is not reactionary to situations of this life. The goodness of God is a steady stream of truth, clearing the way before us to experience the great glory of God. I have learned the two go hand in hand: glory and goodness. When you ask for one in this pair, you will experience the other, too.

Goodness before Glory

Moses experienced the duo of goodness and glory when he and God had a conversation in the book of Exodus:

> And he said, "Please, show me Your glory." Then He said, "I will make all My goodness pass before you, and I will proclaim the name of the LORD before you. I will be gracious to whom I will be gracious, and I will have compassion on whom I will have compassion." But He said, "You cannot see My face; for no man shall see Me, and live." And the LORD said, "Here is a place by Me, and you shall stand on the rock. So it shall be, while My glory passes by, that I will put you in the cleft of the rock, and will cover you with My hand while I pass by. Then I will take away My hand, and you shall see My back; but My face shall not be seen." (Exod. 33:18–23 NKJV)

Moses initially asks to see God's glory. When we think of the glory of God, we often think of something external, some physical bright shining manifestation of God. But when Moses has this request, he is really asking to see God from the inside out. He wants to know the very depths of God. And while God eventually gets to the glory, he first says, "I will make all My goodness pass before you..."

Why was it necessary for his goodness to pass before Moses prior to Moses seeing God's glory? Moses only knew to ask for what he thought was the deepest part of God. But God wanted to show Moses so much more. God knew Moses, the leaders that would follow him, and all of the Israelites would experience the glory of God in many different ways. But sometimes, those victories would come at a cost: a cost of complete obedience, blind faith, and a long journey. God would be sure his glory would be exposed in all the earth. But if Moses was going to stay faithful, if Israel was going to remain faithful, they needed to grasp that God is good. Goodness is at the very core of who he is; and out of his goodness comes glory. So, the goodness of God passing before Moses, prior to him seeing God's glory, was to reveal who God really is. He is good, and his goodness would go before Moses and the Israelites, paving the way for the glory of God to be revealed.

Following this life-changing encounter, God gave Moses straightforward and specific instructions for his people. God revealed meeting times with him, set boundaries, compelled their hearts for giving, and instructed them on how to build and create the tabernacle, how and what to sacrifice, and how and when to cleanse, to name just a few. The instructions were clear, detailed, and very precise. This is why it was important for Moses to experience goodness before glory. Moses needed to know that goodness is who God is, that in all the process, in all the instruction, in the pain and labor, God is still so good, and that his glory would soon rest on them.

Unseen Goodness

The words of the Lord passed from one generation to the next, and Joshua stepped into his destiny to lead the Israelites into the promised land. While the promised land was flowing with milk and honey, a lot of *-ites* inhabited the area. The promise was before them, but there was also a problem. There were battles to be won if the Israelites wanted to bask in the promise. Too often, we want the promise without the fight that comes with it. And when we see things aren't going to be as easy as we hoped, when things get a bit difficult, our response is to question God and ultimately question his goodness.

God began to speak to Joshua about what was ahead of them:

> So Joshua said to the children of Israel, "Come here, and hear the words of the LORD your God." And Joshua said, "By this you shall know that the living God *is* among you, and *that* He will without fail drive out from before you the Canaanites and the Hittites and the Hivites and the Perizzites and the Girgashites and the Amorites and the Jebusites: Behold, the ark of the covenant of the Lord of all the earth is crossing over before you into the Jordan. Now therefore, take for yourselves twelve men from the tribes of Israel, one man from every tribe. And it shall come to pass, as soon as the soles of the feet of the priests who bear the ark of the LORD, the Lord of all the earth, shall rest in the waters of the Jordan, *that* the waters of the Jordan shall be cut off, the waters that come down from upstream, and they shall stand as a heap." (Josh. 3:9–13 NKJV)

God told the Israelites he would drive out the *-ites* from before them, but first they had to cross the Jordan River. The priests would need to step into the water with the ark, and then the waters would be cut off. They would then have to stand there and hold the ark while all of Israel crossed through the Jordan River. Following the crossing of the Jordan, the Israelites built a twelve-stone memorial. Here's the key: when the Israelites stepped into the river in obedience, it propelled the goodness of God to move before them. The Scripture continues to say:

> So it was, when all the kings of the Amorites who *were* on the west side of the Jordan, and all the kings of the Canaanites who *were* by the sea, heard that the LORD had dried up the waters of the Jordan from before the children of Israel until we had crossed over, that their heart melted; and there was no spirit in them any longer because of the children of Israel. (Josh. 5:1 NKJV)

Joshua couldn't see it, the Israelites couldn't see it, but the goodness of God moved before them, word got around, and the hearts of the *-ites* kings melted, leaving them hopeless. All this was happening while God was asking Joshua to circumcise all those who had not yet cut that covenant with God. God had spoken that he would go before the Israelites and drive out the inhabitants of the land, but acts of obedience were required, coupled with hearts of trust that the goodness of God would go before them.

Now Joshua and the Israelites had obeyed, crossed the Jordan, built a memorial, and were circumcised, and they were ready to enjoy the promised land because God had gone before them and had driven out the *-ites*, right? Not quite. Joshua then found himself entering the promised land with a battle before him. I can imagine it would have been easy for Joshua to question God, wondering what all the talk of "going before and driving them out" was about now that they were headed into battle. We place expectations on what the goodness of God should do and what it should look like, especially when we think God will go before us and remove all the hardship. God had said he would go before the Israelites, but then they were preparing for battle. The goodness of God goes before us, but that does not mean we will not face hardship; it does not mean we won't have to go to war, but it does mean the glory that follows will be worth the fight. We must trust that the goodness of God has gone before us, even when it doesn't look like it.

Joshua now faced a city surrounded by giant walls and occupied by -ites. But Joshua trusted the word of the Lord—that he had gone before them—and so he rallied the troops to take their first victory at Jericho. God gave them clear and unusual instruction, just as he had done with their forefathers. The marching around the city, the being mocked, the not getting to keep anything after they defeated the city could seem like a lot to ask of the Israelites. But what if, because God had shown Moses his goodness before his glory, and Moses had shared this with Joshua, Joshua doesn't question unusual instruction when he receives it? What if he trusts that the heart of God is really good, and if they want to experience the glory of victory, they must obey the heart of God and his good instruction that has gone before them?

God had so much more in store for the Israelites than what they could see with their own eyes or conceive in their hearts and minds. It would have been easy for Joshua and the Israelites to take matters into their own hands and go to war the only way they knew how. And it might have seemed like a lot of riches and beautiful things lay inside the city of Jericho. But there was so much more in store than what they could imagine. Joshua had to trust in the character and the goodness of God. He had to trust that goodness had gone before them, and the glory to follow was more than what the city could offer.

Goodness of Jesus

The goodness of God continually goes before us, even when we can't see it—we must trust that he is doing what he said he would do. It may not look like we think it should, it might not seem like anything is happening at all, but goodness is going before us, making a way. We all want to experience the goodness and glory God has to offer us in this life, but we don't want to have to follow, or perhaps we are hesitant to follow, the instruction that comes with them. In that mindset, we are missing the heart of God, we are missing his goodness, and therefore we don't experience his magnificent glory as we should. We doubt the goodness of God because this life has seemed to fail us, and then we miss his glory. But if we would readjust our vision and see that goodness is who God is, and his goodness goes before us, then we could walk in blind faith and allow the glory of God to overwhelm us even in this fallen world.

Here is the good news. The Old Testament went before the New Testament, testifying to the goodness that comes before glory. Then within the New Testament, we see the goodness of salvation break forth so that all the world could experience the glory of God.

We first see this happen in the birth of Jesus. The stars were placed in the sky as part of the day and night, set for times and season. And as a new season of goodness was birthed into this world, so a star shone bright for all to see, marking a new season before them. The magi began to travel to see if this was really the Messiah. They followed the star, "And behold, the star they had seen in the east went on before them, until it came to rest over the place where the Child was" (Matt. 2:9).

The goodness of God that had been placed in the sky for times and seasons went before those seeking the messiah and guided them to their salvation, their Goodness. "When they saw the star, they rejoiced exceedingly with great gladness" (Matt. 2:10). The goodness of a star led them to the goodness of salvation, allowing them to experience the glory of God.

We see goodness and glory in Jesus's life. As Jesus walked this earth, he continually went before his disciples and before the broken, bound, and blind, and brought goodness to their lives so everyone he encountered could experience the great glory of God. Goodness is taken to a new level as we see this concept on display not only in Jesus's life but also in his death. Jesus submits himself to the will of the Father and willingly goes to the cross. Remember, just as it was with Moses and the Israelites, sometimes the instruction we are given seems to be too much, too difficult, too strange, but if we want to experience God's glory, we have to submit to the instruction of goodness that goes before us.

Jesus went to the garden of Gethsemane to pray. And we read of Jesus having a very real and vulnerable conversation with God while there: "Going a little farther, He fell face down and prayed, saying, 'My Father, if it is possible, let this cup pass from Me! Yet not as I will, but as You will'" (Matt. 26:39).

The act of obedience seemed to be too much to bear, but Jesus left his human will there and embraced the will of the Father, initiating the ultimate act of goodness going before us. Jesus died on the cross, was buried in the tomb, and then was raised back to life three days later. That is pretty glorious, but glory was just getting started.

Jesus, our goodness, went before us, paved the way on the cross, and rose again. But Jesus, our goodness, wasn't done yet. He left the tomb and went before his disciples to Galilee (Matt. 28:7;

Mark 16:7). Jesus revealed the glory of his resurrection to them there. He continued to perform miracles, signs, and wonders, and then imparted to the disciples the calling to reach the world, to spread the good news (Mark 16:15; John 30:30). Again, this task might have seemed overwhelming, but the goodness of God, Jesus, had gone before them and revealed to them the great power that would unleash the glory of God. The disciples had to now trust the goodness of God that would go before them, as demonstrated so many times before, so the glory of God could be revealed to the world.

And finally, before Jesus ascended to heaven, he gave his disciples clear instruction not to depart from Jerusalem:

> And being assembled together with *them*, He commanded them not to depart from Jerusalem, but to wait for the Promise of the Father, "which," He *said*, "you have heard from Me; for John truly baptized with water, but you shall be baptized with the Holy Spirit not many days from now." (Acts 1:4–5 NKJV)

Jesus, their goodness, had left, and the disciples in Jerusalem, having been instructed not to leave, are now waiting. Had they not trusted the goodness of God, Jesus, waiting for something unknown in Jerusalem would have seemed ridiculous. But because they trusted and knew that the heart of God was good, they knew goodness had gone before them, and so they waited for the glory that followed.

Jesus told his followers there was more to come, but for that to happen, he needed to go away. "I tell you the truth," said Jesus, "It is to your advantage that I go away; for if I do not go away, the Helper will not come to you; but if I depart, I will send Him to you" (John 16:7 NKJV). As they waited, suddenly there came a sound like wind that filled the room, and each of them in the upper room were filled with the Holy Spirit. While it seemed goodness had left, it had only gone before them so they could experience the glory of the Holy Spirit. That glory, that power, enabled each of them to walk out their faith and reach the world around them. But that glory had to have the foundation of trust that came from their Absolute Goodness that had gone before them.

Just as he did with the disciples, God invites us to walk in the power of the Holy Spirit. When we accept Christ, we receive the ultimate goodness of God into our lives. But just as it happened with Moses, where there is goodness, there is glory. So it is with us too. God desires for us to live submitted to the Holy Spirit, allowing the power and glory of God to flow in us and through us, enabling us to offer this world the same glory and power.

I experienced the goodness of salvation when I was a young girl. I was only five years old when I first invited Jesus into my heart. Young and pure, the goodness of God captured my heart. Jesus was always the love in my heart. But as life happened and got a bit messy and a little unclear, so did my faith. I always loved Jesus, but I didn't understand that more was to follow the goodness that captured my heart. It took a while for me to grasp that there was a glory that followed the goodness of salvation. But one warm summer night at a church camp would forever change me. Seven years after asking Jesus into my life, I experienced the glory of the Holy Spirit unlike ever before.

That night at a simple yet powerful church camp, with my heart open, I received what the Holy Spirit wanted to give to me. We must trust not in what the world says about goodness and glory, but we must trust in what the Word says about Jesus and the Holy Spirit. We by faith believe in Jesus our goodness, and by faith we should accept and trust in the gifts of the Holy Spirit and the glory that comes with them.

Continual Goodness

Hebrews 7:25 tells us Jesus is sitting at the right hand of the Father, making intercession for you and me. We never have to wonder where Jesus is because we know he has gone to the Father ahead of us. No matter the pain, the grief, the circumstance, the uncertainty, we know that goodness is before us and is seated on the throne in victory, interceding for you and me. Goodness went before and is continually going before, making a way for us to experience God's glory. Jesus has gone before to prepare a place for us so that we can forever live in the glory of God. We, like the magi, must keep our eyes fixed and ready, looking to the sky for our Goodness to return to take us to glory.

The goodness of God and his glory are a dynamic duo. Moses so boldly asked for what he probably thought was the most extravagant thing to ask for, but God is always so much bigger than that. Moses asked for glory, but God extended goodness and glory in a package deal that we can see stream throughout the Word and into our own lives. The goodness of God is continually going before us. It is making a way when there seems to be no way. It is preparing the waters to part; it is melting the hearts of our enemies; it is our salvation. And goodness's partner glory is waiting to lavish us with every step of obedience we take in faith. Even when we can't see it, we must trust that the goodness of God has gone before us and his glory is following right behind.

Chapter Three Reflection

1. Is there something God is asking you to do, but you feel hesitant about stepping out? Whatever it is, I encourage you to submit your will to his and trust that goodness has gone before you and glory is on its way.

2. The Holy Spirit has good gifts for you so that he can use you in a mighty way to impact the kingdom. Have you experienced the power of the Holy Spirit and allowed those gifts to be used through you?

four

My Goodness Follows

As believers in Jesus Christ, you and I need to be also trusting that the goodness and mercy of God are following our every step. We need to be similarly confident and comforted, believing that every day of our lives, these two friends of David are with us for every step of life's journey.

—Dr. Steven J. Lawson

HAVE YOU EVER FELT LIKE YOU WERE BEING FOLlowed? Your body feels there is someone who is close behind, and your mind starts to sense someone is pursuing you. This feeling happens every single day. I move from room to room in my house and always feel as if there is someone close behind. I would start to think that it is weird, but I guess it's not since it always turns out to be one of my three boys. Children are relentless followers.

Children can teach us the best lessons. They desire to follow those in front of them. While it can get somewhat irritating after a long day, their relentless pursuit is just a sign of their affection and love. Mommas know what I am talking about; kids will follow you into the restroom at home, while all you're wanting is a moment of peace. They love you enough to pursue you to the potty. While it's charming that my boys want to follow me, their continual pursuit isn't on the list of my favorite things.

We live in a world where we don't want people following us around, but we want followers. We want people to like our social media posts. We want people to comment on our cute Instagram photo. We desire all the followers, but we want them at a distance. And in this process of seeking followers, we miss the one who relentlessly follows us. When our lives come to a screeching halt, if our focus has been on gaining followers rather than on the one following us, we surely miss his goodness. We must grasp the concept that the goodness of God is relentlessly pursuing and following closely behind us as our provision.

Surely Goodness

God called David a man after his own heart (1 Sam. 13:14; Acts 13:22). Those words forever labeled David as one who relentlessly pursued God through survival, sin, sacrifice, and success. Though David wrote many words, some of his most famous are found in Psalms 23. You can find excellent studies, sermons, and books over this specific chapter of the Bible, but I want to look at one specific verse: "Surely goodness and mercy will follow me all the days of my life, and I will dwell in the House of *Adonai* forever" (Ps. 23:6).

David insistently pursued God, all while God pursued David. Before David took his place on the throne as king of Israel, King Saul ruled the people. Saul fell into the trap of jealousy at the thought of David replacing him on the throne. This rage sent Saul and David into a cat and mouse act throughout the countryside. Saul, determined with everything in him to kill David, sought

David's life time and time again, causing David to run away from the throne to ensure survival.

Life has a way of doing this to us—making us feel like we aren't moving in the right direction. God will reveal your purpose, give you a promise, but soon you will find your entire life has flipped upside down, and you appear to be moving in the opposite direction. David served near the throne he would one day sit on. He played his harp with all his might, with all his integrity, patiently waiting for the fulfillment of God's promise. David was supposed to be moving from shepherd of the field to king of the people. But in an instant, David found himself running for his life. How many of you can relate? I know I can. God plants a promise deep in the soil of our hearts, and we feel so close to the fulfillment of the promise when suddenly life throws a curveball, sending us into what seems to be the opposite direction.

Fading Promises

Maybe you worked extremely hard for the promotion. Those over you at work dropped hints that you would receive the next promotion. You prayed, and God gave you peace, Scripture, and confirmation that he would elevate you. The next thing you know, you have been fired and now spun around to face what feels like the opposite direction of the promise.

Maybe you and your spouse have been trying to get pregnant. You have prayed and clung to the promises of God in his Word. In sweet sleep, you have dreamt of the children that would fill your house. But the doctor tells you that you will never be able to have children. Then maybe you do get pregnant only to lose your sweet baby. And life suddenly shifts in what seems like the opposite direction of the promise.

Joseph surely felt similar. Genesis recounts his dreams of ruling over his brothers and wearing his coat of many colors, only to find himself in a pit and sold into slavery by his brothers. He was later promoted, though still a slave, to oversee Potiphar's house. I'm sure thoughts that God was restoring him to the place of his dreams lingered in his mind. He was so close to the fulfillment of God's promise, but then he found himself in prison, the exact opposite direction of the promise (Gen. 37–50).

God will give us promises. His promises are "yes" and our response through him is "amen" (2 Cor. 1:20). But life has a way of making us feel like we are moving in the opposite direction of yes. David had been close to death at the hands of Saul. And Saul had been close to death at the hands of David. During this back-and-forth, up-and-down, David seemed to move in every direction except toward the promise. It's in those life-shaking moments when yes is nowhere near that we miss the goodness of God. Our hearts quickly move to doubt and question instead of resting in the provision and pursuit of God's goodness.

David wrote, "Surely goodness and mercy will follow me all the days of my life" (Ps. 23:6). In our pursuit of the promise God has placed on our lives, we must cling to the promise that God's goodness is surely following. But when life takes a sharp turn, sadly, doubt and questions muddle our vision of goodness.

Picture in your mind the goodness of God following us, relentlessly chasing after us. Then, when our life suddenly spins us in the opposite direction of the promise, it causes us to run smack dab into the goodness of God. Remember I said my boys like to follow me everywhere? In their pursuit of me, if I suddenly stop and turn around, I will run into them. The same is true with the goodness of God. Goodness is surely following us all the days of our life. And just when we think life has turned us in the opposite direction, instead of seeing doubt, we must embrace the collision with goodness and allow it to envelop our hearts and minds.

Children of God

The children of God experienced this goodness following them through their years of travel in the wilderness. The Hebrew people spent hundreds of years in slavery under the rule of Egypt. And we know God promised to bring them out from under the hand of Pharaoh. They had the promise of God written on their hearts and minds. The promise of freedom in a land flowing with milk and honey. God miraculously delivered them from Egypt, from the house of bondage. After the Israelites escaped the grip of Pharaoh by the strong hand of God, they wandered in the wilderness for a while. There was a route for them to reach their destination that appeared short in distance but would have been hard on their hearts. So God guided them with a cloud by day and fire by night. And while they were following the goodness of God that guided them, the enemy began to follow the Israelites.

We experience this often in life. We pursue and trust our good Father, yet we feel the pressure of the enemy following us. The enemy will relentlessly pursue us, but we must trust that the same goodness going before us will be the same goodness following us.

"Then the angel of God, who went before the camp of Israel, moved and went behind them. Also the pillar of cloud moved from in front and stood behind them" (Exod. 14:19). The goodness of God moved before his children, and just when it seemed the enemy would overtake them, goodness followed, delivering them from the enemy and propelling them forward. Their God wondrously parted the sea, and they crossed untouched. What a spiritual high, right? Then suddenly, the Hebrews found themselves on the other side of bondage, wandering in the wilderness—this was not the promise. The promise was freedom, milk, honey, a comfortable life. Yet they found themselves tired, hungry, and thirsty.

Anytime I read the grumblings of the Israelites in the wilderness, I am tempted to roll my eyes. At times, it can seem like they are some of the most impatient and moody people. The Holy Spirit quickly reminds me that I am not that different. So there the Hebrews were, wandering in the wilderness with grumbling hearts and stomachs and thirsty mouths and minds, when God responds. God tells Moses in Exodus 17 to strike the rock, and water will come out, then the people can drink. Then, in Numbers 20, God tells Moses to speak to the rock and water will come out. This time, Moses disobeyed. He chose not to speak, but once again struck the rock and water came out. God wasn't pleased with Moses, but that's not the focus for the moment. Let's focus on that rock.

Twice, the Hebrews were thirsty, and God gave them water from a rock. Let's think about this for a moment. Was this just any rock? Was the rock huge? I feel like the rock would need to have been pretty significant in size to meet the need of all the thirsty Hebrews. In the New Testament, Paul gives a little insight into this miracle rock: "And all drank the same spiritual drink—for they were drinking from a spiritual rock that followed them, and the Rock was Messiah" (1 Cor. 10:4).

Paul writes some pretty big truths in that short verse. He tells us that the rock the Hebrews drank from not only contained water; he tells us that rock was Jesus. Picture this: as the children of God wandered in the desert, there was a rock that followed them. Everywhere they went, the rock went. Again, the question of the size of the rock comes to mind. We know this was an actual rock because they could see it and water came from it. But Paul also tells us that rock was Jesus. Jesus is our chief cornerstone, the bedrock of truth, and the living water that never runs dry (Eph. 2:20; John 4:14). The Hebrews wandering in the wilderness, seemingly against the direction of the promise, find the rock that never stopped following them. Just when they thought they wouldn't see the promise, when they couldn't go any longer and felt their lives coming to an end, living water broke forth from the goodness that followed them.

When David wrote, "surely goodness and mercy shall follow me," I can't help but think that he was picturing the goodness of God that followed those who had gone before him. David surely treasured the miraculous history of his forefathers deep in his heart. He would have been well aware of the rock that followed and provided for the Hebrews in the wilderness. David, still moving in what seemed like the opposite direction of his promise, remembered that the goodness of God is forever pursuing him just like those who went before him.

The children of God had a physical rock that followed them, so I think it would have been easy for them to remember the goodness of God. We don't have an actual rock that follows us, so when our lives come to a halt and we suddenly turn in the other direction, we won't crash into a boulder. We should strive to resemble David in our actions, encouraging ourselves and reminding ourselves that our goodness is pursuing us and wants to give us living water as refreshment amid our chaos.

God knows the things we will face in this life that appear to be in contrast to his promise. But if we will take time to allow the ever-pursing goodness of God to come crashing into our chaos, there will be new glory found.

Late Goodness

Jesus made some good friends during his time of ministry. A couple of his close friends happened to be Mary, Martha, and Lazarus from Bethany. Jesus received word that Lazarus, his good friend, laid very ill. Jesus lovingly and graciously replied with encouraging news: "This sickness will not end in death. No, it is for God's glory so that God's Son may be glorified through it" (John 11:4 NIV).

Great news! What a promise—Lazarus is sick, but he isn't going to die. Jesus and his disciples stayed where they were for a couple of days more. Then Jesus told the disciples they were going to Bethany because Lazarus has died. Wait! Hold on. Jesus had just said this would not end in death. He gave his word. Suddenly, Lazarus moved in the complete opposite direction of the promise, from life to death. Reconciling the promises of God and the reality in front of us is difficult to do. Questions start to arise, thoughts begin to wander, and doubt starts to grow. Here in these moments, when life appears to oppose the promises, uncertainty rises and starts to cloud the goodness of God.

But we must never forget the promise David wrote—"Surely goodness and mercy will follow me"—even when it doesn't look like it. Even when the death of a promise seems to hover, we must trust that we will see the goodness of God, which relentlessly chases us, come crashing onto the scene, flooding our lives with living waters.

Jesus continued to make his way to Bethany with his disciples. I don't know about you, but when I read this text, I start to feel like Jesus needs to hurry. Lazarus was dead, Mary and Martha were grieving, and it seems like Jesus was moving at a leisurely pace. And when Jesus and the disciples arrived, they found that Lazarus wasn't just dead, but had been in the tomb for four days. I've heard many songs sung and many messages preached on God's perfect timing—things like, "When it seems he is four days late, Jesus is right on time," and, "He's an on-time God." While those are true, it's challenging to cling to clichés attached to the Word when your world is crumbling around you. When a building comes crumbling to the ground, a cloud of dust billows as millions of minuscule particles rise like smoke all around where the building once stood. This image comes to mind when I think about moments in our lives that cause us to come to a standstill. As our lives seem to crumble to the ground, a haze of what should have been starts to rise around us. Our vision becomes cloudy, and seeing the goodness of God becomes difficult.

The phrase "This will not end in death," facing the tension of the words "been in the tomb for four days," seems to be breeding ground for questions and doubt. Mary and Martha's world suddenly came to a halt where grief consumed them. The cloud of grief surrounded them, but then we read, "When Martha heard that Jesus was coming, she went out to meet him" (John 11:20 NIV).

Martha heard Jesus was coming. She heard the good news. She heard the sound of goodness on its way. As sure as grief and doubt began clouding her vision, she allowed her heart to trust that goodness was surely following close behind. Even when she couldn't see, she listened, and then she heard. She got up and ran toward the goodness that followed her, even in the middle of pain and grief.

Just when they thought life ended, the goodness that never stops following showed up on the scene. Jesus, our goodness, Mary and Martha's goodness, followed closely. It must have seemed like the promises of God were not going to come to pass. It surely felt like life would never be normal again. I imagine it felt like goodness missed the mark. But even when it seems like goodness missed us, like goodness didn't make good on its promise, we can rest assured it will come crashing in at the right moment.

Jesus came to do an absolute miracle. He didn't want to heal Lazarus while he was sick. He didn't want to bring him back to life right after he died. Jesus wanted Lazarus dead—wrapped-in-cloth, sealed-in-the-tomb dead. Then when Jesus and all his goodness showed up, it would bring the glory of God. Our promises may seem to be dead and mummified and sealed away in a tomb in our hearts. But you can rest assured that the goodness of God is relentlessly following you. And when your life comes to a halt, God's goodness comes crashing in, reviving the promise and bringing a new glory. Just like with the children of God in the wilderness: when they stopped to seek the rock that had been following them, water met their needs. And only when there was no hope for the promise of Lazarus's life did living water break forth from Jesus's mouth, bringing the promise back to life.

We must find ourselves not just seeing the goodness of God that is following us, not just hearing it, but letting the living water flow over our lives. David did this by encouraging his heart with Scripture, and this is what we must do too. We need the words of Jesus to wash over us in the wilderness, in our mess, and must let the refreshing power of goodness bring the glory of God.

Sudden Goodness

Brad and I have experienced the goodness of God relentlessly following us too many times to count and probably more times than we will ever know. But one specific season comes to mind. Brad and I were so blessed to have purchased a home when we were first married. We lived in our first house for a couple of years and brought our first two boys home from the hospital to that quaint home.

About a year after we brought our second boy home, an opportunity arose for us to purchase another home. We prayed about it and knew God said we could do this. It was a fixer-upper, and we were so excited to flip this house. We fixed up the second home and moved in and decided to rent out our first home. All the renovations were complete, and we made a new home. (Praise break, because Brad and I still loved each other after the renovation.)

Reality check: we now had two mortgages, two boys, and one job. God had provided, and life was moving ahead smoothly. Then one day, our sweet second, Collin, got sick. It was a rough couple of weeks until he finally seemed to start feeling better. One night while rocking him to sleep, loving on my sweet boy, I felt swollen knots on the back of his head. It freaked me out. I knew lymph nodes could swell, but I had never felt anything like this before. So the next morning, I called his pediatrician, booked an appointment, and took him in. The doctor seemed very concerned, so we were quickly sent to have extensive blood work done. The hospital drew a lot of blood out of our little boy. Then it was a waiting game.

A couple of days later while driving home from running a couple of errands, my cell phone rang. It was the doctor's office. My heart wanted to be scared, but I believed I would receive a good report. I answered and said, "Hello?" Typically, when the boys' doctor's office calls to relay results from a test, it is a nurse or the physician's assistant who gives the report. I fully expected to hear one of their sweet voices when, to my surprise, I heard the doctor's voice say, "Mrs. Sugg." My heart sank. "Morgan," he continued, "we got Collin's blood work back. It doesn't look good." The doctor went on to tell me that the blood work and tests appeared to indicate that Collin had some form of the dreaded "C" word: cancer. My heart sank, and my world came to a halt.

That day, my world started to feel like one of those imploding buildings that come crashing down. It would be that same week that my husband would lose his job. The dust of our crumbling world seemed to be rising higher and higher: two mortgages, two boys—one who appeared to be very ill—and no source of income. Life felt like it stopped, our vision blurred, the promises of God faded, and goodness seemed distant.

The week we would never forget came to an end, and the weekend began. Brad and I were at a loss, not sure what to do next or how to move forward. Our vision was now skewed by the cloud of doubt that pressed against the promises God had placed in our hearts. But just as it happened with Martha, when she couldn't see goodness, she heard it. The goodness of God was surely following; we couldn't see goodness at the moment, but we heard it coming.

That weekend as Brad and I were driving to church, I heard the spirit of God speak to me. He told me to give one thousand dollars as an offering at church. I heard God, and I said, "Okay." I was hesitant to tell Brad what God had said because we didn't have much more than a thousand in the bank. But I talked to Brad, and he instantly agreed we would give. In the story of Lazarus, when Martha hears Jesus is coming, she goes to him. Jesus and Martha engaged in very real conversation. But at the end of the conversation, Jesus asks Martha one last question: "'Do you believe this?' She said to Him, 'Yes, Lord, I believe'" (John 11:26–27 NKJV).

While God and I had a different conversation, its essence is the same. Jesus wanted to know if Martha believed he would make good on his promises. God wanted to see if I trusted him to make good on his promises. My heart and obedience said, "Yes, Lord, I believe." The moment I allowed my heart to hear God in the midst of chaos, I opened the door to see the goodness of God following close behind like the rock that followed the children of God.

The weekend ended, and a new week arose. That Monday morning, Brad and I received a check for one thousand dollars, due to someone else's obedience. That day, Collin broke out in a rash. The doctor said he now had scarlet fever, his new blood work came back normal, and our boy would be perfectly fine. And a job offer came in beyond what Brad and I could have imagined.

The goodness of God followed close behind as our life felt as if it would never be put back together. But like a flood, living water broke forth, and the goodness of God came crashing in, clearing away the cloud of doubt and beginning the fulfillment of his promises.

The rock of our salvation is continually following us. It is never far behind and never stops pursuing us. It doesn't matter if we are in the middle of a wilderness, if the enemy is insistently chasing us, or if our promises seem to be dying in front of us. We can rest assured that the rock of goodness, Jesus, will show up on the scene, making good on the promises of God. The Hebrews wandered the desert for forty years. Lazarus was dead for four days. Whether four days or forty years, it all feels the same when our lives come to a standstill. But we can trust that surely goodness and mercy are following us all the days of our lives. The rock of our salvation is pursuing us and will send rivers of living water to flow into our mess and bring life to the promises planted in our hearts. We must let the peace of knowing the goodness of God is continually following us captivate our hearts.

Chapter Four Reflection

1. Have you ever felt like life is moving in the opposite direction of the promises of God?

2. In those moments, do you start to frantically figure out how to fix what has happened, or do you pause and embrace the collision with the goodness of living water that has been following you?

3. Write down the promises God has spoken to you, and then, like what happened during Martha's and Jesus's conversation, proclaim that you believe Jesus will do what he has promised.

five

My Goodness Is Guidance

Guidance, like all God's acts of blessing under the covenant of grace, is a sovereign act. Not merely does God will to guide us in the sense of showing us his way, that we may tread it; he wills also to guide us in the more fundamental sense of ensuring that, whatever happens, whatever mistakes we may make, we shall come safely home. Slippings and strayings there will be, no doubt, but the everlasting arms are beneath us; we shall be caught, rescued, restored. This is God's promise; this is how good he is.

—J. I. Packer

One cold February, Brad and I drove from Texas to New Mexico for a short ski trip. The weather was beautiful as we drove the ten hours to our family cabin. We hit the slopes and enjoyed the beauty of God's creation. After a couple of days, the time came to head back home to rescue and thank my mom for watching our boys.

As we packed the car to leave, we decided to take a different route home. The new course would shave a decent amount of time off our ordinary trip. With the car loaded and the day getting late, we hit the road.

As we trekked eastbound, the sun started to set behind us and the trip moved along smoothly. Suddenly, the wind began to blow, and snow started to fall. Now, this wasn't anything Brad and I hadn't experienced. We both had traveled in snow, so we weren't too worried—until the snow was so thick that we couldn't see more than four to five feet in front of the car.

We moved from evening into the night, and the only light around us came from the two beams shooting from the front of our SUV. This different route was one less traveled, far from a major highway. There was no one around and very few signs to guide us. Smartphones were a new and hot commodity, leaving iMaps and Waze almost unheard of at the time. We traveled with our trustworthy black, square Garmin sticking out from the windshield.

That small GPS screen displayed the only guidance we had through the storm. Due to limited visibility, we relied on the GPS map to tell us when the road was going to curve, which direction it would turn, and how sharp the turn would be. That GPS was our only guide through the middle of that nighttime snowstorm. On that beautiful snowy drive, Brad and I only had the guidance of our GPS. Without that device, becoming lost or wrecking were strong possibilities. That map guided us to the safety of our home.

We all need guidance. Life takes unexpected turns, and sudden storms will blow our way. But through it all, we have guidance. The goodness of God is moving with us and guiding us, helping us find our way.

Season and Storms

There is a joke in Texas that we can experience four seasons in one week. Even as I write this, in mid-July, we are all rejoicing that a cold front is going to blow through, dropping the temperature to eighty degrees. While we joke about our weather, it is a very real story. Our weather is all over the place. It's not a surprise in the least to experience rain one day, scorching heats the next, then the possibility of tornadoes, followed by a beautiful day in the low eighties. While this type of crazy weather pattern does not happen often, we Texans do endure the most unsettled weather. There is one season that I believe everyone anticipates the most—fall.

I think fall is so loved around here because we experience excruciatingly hot summers. After facing temperatures that are hot in June, extreme in July, brutal in August, and lingeringly high in September, come October 1, we want it to be fall. There is a little celebration that happens because we know a reprieve is on the horizon. But there is always a chance that when we check the fourteen-day weather forecast coming into October 1, we might see that we are going to hit ninety degrees on October 2. I don't know about you, but at the beginning of September, I start anticipating fall. I put pumpkins out around my home. I switch the pillows on my sofas to oranges and browns. I have my fall candles burning, filling our home with the scent of apple cider, and I rejoice when I can get a pumpkin spiced latte. I prep and anticipate for that cool wind to start blowing. Only to find on October 2, the temperature will still hit ninety degrees.

How many of us experience seasons like this in our lives? We find ourselves in a brutal season where we feel like the hot sun wearies our souls. We feel exhausted and almost dehydrated. Like one does on a hot summer day, drinking a lot of water and finding time to swim in a refreshing pool, you fill your heart and mind with the Word of God and worship. But you find yourself waking up the next day with the same pressure, the same problem, the same heat beating down. You look ahead, knowing the season will change, and you find strength and peace in this. You know God wants to lead you forward to something greater, but right now, you are still facing the battle. The heat is still on. How many of you know that every season and every storm is different? Some storms are short-lived, while others seem like they will never end.

One spring Sunday, Brad and I locked up the church after service along with a few other staff members. As we all exited the building and walked to our cars, the light blue sky turned to a beautiful and gloomy dark turquoise and gray. We stood in the parking lot long enough to snap a quick picture of the massive storm cloud that headed our direction. We all sat down in our respective vehicles and started to drive to the restaurant, our next meeting place. While we were driving, the storm moved over us, the rain and pea-sized hail blew hard through the town as the wind gusted, uprooting trees and knocking down branches. The storm was rough, massive, and destructive. But it only lasted fifteen minutes. As quickly as the crystal blue sky had disappeared, it reappeared. We sometimes face storms that appear quickly, hurt us, but then fade just as fast.

Then some storms never seem to end. I grew up in the West Texas town of Midland. The weather there was fickle but mostly hot and dry. I think that during my entire time in Midland, we were in a drought. There was never quite enough water, never quite enough rain to bring us out of the dry season. While drought isn't a typical storm, it is one that can be long lasting, and you never know when it may come to an end. Growing up, praying for rain was a routine and almost daily request for my family. We knew God would provide, but we didn't know when. There are storms we face that linger for years, even a decade or two. We

My Goodness Is Guidance

pray daily for provision, we know God will come through, but we don't know when.

The storms of this life vary in size, length, and type. But no matter the storm, our hearts feel desperate to hear the voice of God. In the middle of crazy weather, we listen carefully to the meteorologist on our televisions, we watch the radar on our phones, and we check social media. We do this in our efforts to stay up-to-date and know what our next move should be.

- Do we need to go to the closet and cover-up for protection?
- Do we need to board up our house and evacuate?
- Do we need to limit our water usage?
- Do we need to go to the store and fill up with the necessities?

We ask and we listen for guidance on how to weather the storm we are facing. The same should be true when we face storms of this life.

- Our hearts should tune in to our Father.
- Our minds should be searching for his heart.
- Our ears tune in to hear his voice.

Too many times in the middle of the storm, we become frantic. Amid our chaos, we pray, beg, maybe even plead with God, but that's where it ends. We never stop to listen. It does us zero good to turn on the news and see the meteorologist speaking and not listen and follow the instructions she gives us. During the trial, when we pray, we must listen and obey what God speaks to us.

We will encounter storms in this life; we are not exempt from them. But we serve a God who knows every storm that is coming our way. And just like a meteorologist watches the radar and begins to warn us of the upcoming storms, our Father in heaven is good to warn us and prepare us for the trials of this life. He is never surprised by what lies ahead. And we might be a lot less surprised by some storms if we would do more listening.

Once the meteorologist breaks the news of the weather system headed your way, she begins to give you instructions on how to endure the storm. God is faithful to speak to you. He is faithful to provide you with directions on how to stand in the middle of the trial. A meteorologist will do her best to predict the outcome of the storm, but that's all she can do. But the God we serve, in his great goodness, has seen the end and knows exactly how each trial you face will end. And he is good enough to reveal what you need to make it through the storm, holding on to the promise of knowing that he has the ending already written. You may not know all the details, but he will give you enough for you to embrace the peace that he is in control.

We see God do this for his children as he is delivering them from Egypt. God prepared the Hebrew people through Moses for what was coming their way. Their season was about to change. But before it did, they would have to endure a little longer. God gave Moses instructions on what to do, what to say, and how to survive. God wants to and will do the same for you and me. God's goodness will guide you through the seasons of this life if you tune in and obey.

The Voyage

Paul, the mighty man of God, faced many trials and storms. Acts 27 describes one of his shipwrecks. Paul was a prisoner on board a ship headed for Rome. The weather they faced extended the already long journey. They were sailing against severe winds, causing them to move slowly. Finally, we read where Paul spoke up and told the centurion he could see this voyage was going to be disastrous if they didn't do something different. Paul was a man of God and was filled with the Holy Spirit, which caused him to hear the heart of God. Paul could see a better way for this to end. Paul was concerned not only for his life, but also for the lives of those on board and the cargo too. That cargo was linked to people's livelihoods. When our hearts are inclined to hear God, we begin to see what he wants us to see. Our concern moves from just about us to those around us.

The Holy Spirit gave Paul insight on how to prepare for what was coming. The Lord provided a strategy to Paul on how to prepare and endure what was soon to come. There was a storm coming, whether the ship went to port or kept sailing. The Lord can and will give you insight on how to prepare for the coming storm. Unfortunately, in Paul's case, the pilot's persuasion overrode Paul's instruction, and the centurion ordered the ship to press on.

The voyage crept on, but before long, hurricane-force winds started to blow, and the northeaster began to wreak havoc. The ship could no longer make its way through the storm and submitted to the winds. As the storm violently battered them, they started throwing the cargo overboard. Then the sun and stars didn't appear for many days, and their hope began to vanish. The men were hungry, they were adrift, and they were almost hopeless when Paul piped up again.

Paul exclaimed that they should have listened to him. I imagine his scold in the midst of the storm brought them to attention. Now that he had their attention, he spoke encouragement to the men. Their hope was faint, and Paul urged them to take heart! *Take heart, and do not fear; this will not end in death.* The Lord had already revealed to Paul that he was going to stand before Caesar. God's goodness revealed the outcome of the storm to Paul.

While trying to scale the sea, Paul and the men in the boat were about to face the storm of all storms. Paul didn't have the news channel or a weather app to reveal to him what was up ahead.

Paul didn't have Twitter to flood him with updates. Paul relied on the Holy Spirit to show him preparations and strategy to endure the storm. The storm was coming, and that wasn't going to change, but God had revealed the next step to Paul. Storms are coming our way, and that isn't going to change. The storms we face don't diminish the goodness of God but rather enhances it. Like a light from a lighthouse for a ship lost at sea, so the goodness of God is revealed. We must keep our hearts turned toward our Father and let the power of the Holy Spirit live in us and bring revelation of the strategy for the storms that may be on the horizon.

While the men didn't heed the words of Paul, we can learn a lesson from them. We have a choice. When the Lord speaks, we have the option to obey. We know the men on the ship didn't listen and found themselves losing hope while lost at sea. When we don't obey, we leave room for the enemy to prey, causing us to lose hope. When we feel like our hope is lost, we question the goodness of God, although we were the ones who failed to follow his Word. God's goodness does not weaken because of our disobedience. It is our hope that begins to fail.

Take heart! Do not fear! God is there to encourage you in the middle of the storm. He is there to reassure you of his presence, goodness, and provision. The angel of the Lord revealed to Paul that there would be no loss of life, and Paul would stand before Caesar. In the middle of your storm, God can reveal the outcome. God didn't tell Paul how they would be saved. God didn't tell Paul what he would face when standing in front of Caesar. God just said they would survive and would make it to Rome. God doesn't always reveal the step-by-step plan at the beginning. He does not always expose the exit from the storm. But he will give you the promise of an exit. God, in his great goodness, is faithful to speak to you in the middle of the storm, to see you through the storm.

Guidance

I experienced this type of revelation and goodness in one of my own trials. I had been working at a wonderful company for several years. I loved where I worked. I loved the people I worked with and the people I worked for. This job was the fulfillment of many promises God had spoken to me years before. But like with everything in our lives, there is a season. Seasons come and go; and with each season, there are unique storms. While I loved my job, I sensed a change in season. I began to feel the stirring of the wind. I could see the clouds start to change directions, and the sky started to darken. So I began to pray. I knew God was calling me to something else, and in my prayers, I would ask God to tell me what was next. And I would hear one word.

I would write that word at the top of my journal but not ask him too many questions about it. If God were going to move me from this job and this place, then it would be wrong of me not to start looking for other jobs. Right? *We have to be proactive. We can't let God think we are lazy.* So, I did what any one of us would have done and started the job search. Not extensively, but just started to put feelers out to gain an idea of what might be available. And I found it. I found the perfect job for me. It was a communications and marketing position at a nonprofit. I thought to myself: *Could it really be true? I would actually get to use my degrees. I would be so good at this!*

One morning during my prayer time, I brought this opportunity to the Lord. I brought it to him like it was new information to him. Isn't it funny how we do that? I poured my heart out over this opportunity and told him how good I would be at this job. And then I asked, "Is this what you would have me do?" I had been totally ignoring the one word that I continually wrote in my journal. And I heard a firm and loving, *No . . . stay.*

I was baffled. I knew the season was changing, and the time was coming to an end. Didn't God want me to move on? One thing we know is that as one season starts to set, there is hope of a new season on the horizon. But sometimes a season lingers longer than we think it should or hoped it would. Though I knew a new season was coming, the seasons don't change just because I want them to. They change when God says. With that, I obeyed and stayed.

I had a consistent word written in my journal of the promise of a new season, but I couldn't force that season to break open. I still had a storm to endure in the present season. God had given me a promise I could cling to in the midst of what was coming in the middle of my *stay* season. I stayed at the job I knew would come to an end, though my heart was longing to possess the promise of a new season.

One morning while my heart longed to move on, but God said to stay, I went deep into prayer. I asked God for a Scripture to cleave to during the final portion of this season. Often when we know we are about to move on, we don't finish our present season strong. There is a common leadership principle that says how we exit one season determines how we enter the next season. As badly as I wanted to move forward, God asked me to stay. I didn't want to be like the men on the ship moving forward even though the man of God said to stay. So, I chose to obey. The choice was mine. I decided to adhere to the word God spoke and stay, but I needed nourishment to finish the season strong.

That morning, I asked God to give me a Scripture. He gave me an entire story. He spoke to my spirit to read the story of Joseph. I turned the pages of my Bible to the book of Genesis. The life of Joseph is spilled out on the pages, chapter after chapter, beginning in chapter 37. The story is a roller coaster for the reader and must have been so much more for Joseph. I quickly picked up my pen and began to write what the Lord was speaking to me.

God revealed the final stretch of this season would be one like the story of Joseph. Joseph was full of promise but had to endure betrayal after betrayal. And I was no different. God had written a promise on my life; but before fulfillment, I would experience betrayal. People who were like family would soon be distant like Joseph's brothers were to him. Someone I loved dearly would be untruthful, like Potiphar's wife. This trial would make me feel like I was in prison, but I needed to pay attention to Joseph's actions while he was in jail. He kept his integrity, served continually, never clinging to unforgiveness but living in love and waiting for God to move him into the next season, with the hope of the promise beating in his heart.

I had a one-word promise beating in my heart, written at the top of numerous pages of my journal, that gave me hope of what lay ahead. I had faith that the season and trial I would face would come to an end. But in the meantime, God knew the storm that was coming my way and revealed it to me. In his goodness, he gave me insight on how to stand during the storm in my season of *stay*.

I obeyed and stayed. Prepared for what was coming, I clung to the Word of God. I followed his instructions as the winds began to blow and the storm started to churn. And just as hurricane-force winds were blowing, one night I had a dream. Like Paul and the men on the ship, the sun wasn't shining, and the stars weren't glowing, and hope was beginning to look grim. Paul spoke up and said, "Take heart!" The dream was like God was saying to me, *Take heart . . . it is almost over.*

The dream, like a lot of dreams we have, was bizarre and left me with wonder. In February 2016, this was the dream I had:

FOREVER IN MY *goodness*

> President Trump was just elected, and I was attending a speech of his, the day after his election. As he walked off the stage, he passed by me. President Trump abruptly stopped. He turned around to me. And in a way that only Trump can do, he pointed his hand at me and said, "You! You're on my team!" Two of the secret service men opened up the velvet rope, and I stepped onto the red carpet and joined the president's team.

I awoke. The dream felt strange but important, hilarious yet intriguing. Friends, don't discount your dreams, especially if you can't shake the feeling they give you! Write them down. Make a journal just for them. God loves to speak to us in many ways, and dreams happen to be one of those avenues. While we sleep, our physical bodies rest, but our spirit is still awake, allowing our natural logic to be lowered. God speaks in parable-type pictures as we dream. Like playing a game of hide and seek, he gives us a clue, but we have the opportunity to seek him for the interpretation through the discernment of the Holy Spirit. The Spirit of God is the giver of dreams (Acts 2:17) and is the interpreter of them (Gen. 40:8). God gives us dreams, and only through seeking him can we understand the picture he painted in our minds. If you have a dream, write it down, pray, and seek him for the interpretation. After I woke up, I wrote the dream down in my journal, prayed for understanding, and let peace settle into my heart.

Fast forward to November 8, 2016. America named Donald Trump as the forty-fifth president of the United States. Wow! I had just dreamt of this nine months earlier. But remember in the dream, the following day, President Trump asked me to come work for him. So, was something that crazy going to happen on November 9th? I didn't go work for Donald Trump the next day, though my life did take a big turn. I was laid off. In the dream, I had gone to work for the most powerful leader of the free world, yet in reality, I was now without a job—but fully available to do whatever God was calling me to do next. Some might say getting laid off is far from what happened in the dream. But I beg to differ.

Remember, God had already spoken a promise of what was coming. I had written that one word down over and over. I wanted to jump ship and leave the season, but God asked me to stay. I obeyed. God gave me his word, revelation, and strategy to endure the storm. He gave me the insight to know that it would end; and through a riddle of a dream, he told me exactly when it would end. Though I didn't know the season would change precisely like this, it wasn't a total surprise to me and definitely not to God. The goodness of God guided me through the storm and season I was in. He spoke Scripture to my heart to cling to and gave me a dream that caused me to seek him in anxious anticipation of what he would reveal.

And instantly, after being laid off, peace settled the storm. The sun began to shine. The stars started to glisten. I began to do that one thing, that one word—*write*. God created the beginning from the end. There is no season he has not seen. No storm will surprise him. The goodness of God brings guidance.

Your Guidance

As Jesus walked through this broken world, we read of his complete dependence on his Father's guidance. He went where the Father said to go. He spoke to the people the Father said to talk to. He ate with those the Father said to dine with. He faced temptation when the Father said to. He died when the Father said to die. He rose when the Father said to rise. Jesus walked through the seasons and storms of this life, and he did it with the guidance of his Father.

Because Jesus is our goodness, we have access to the same guidance from the Father through the Holy Spirit. The Holy Spirit wants to reveal to you the goodness of God through his guidance. He wants to go with you through the fire. He wants to go with you through the rising water. He wants to guide you so that you won't be burned or overtaken. When we allow the Holy Spirit to go with us and bring us out, we are reflecting, just like Jesus, the goodness of our Father to the broken world around us.

- Let the goodness of God speak to you in dreams and visions of the night.
- Let the goodness of God prophesy to your heart and mind.
- Let the goodness of God reveal hidden gems in the Word.
- Let the goodness of God guide you through the seasons of this life, allowing you to be a reflection and reach this hurting world.

God is good to guide you through any season or any storm you enter. The key is to remember that there is no season and there is no storm that overrides the goodness of God. His goodness is an ever-present help. No matter the season or storm, God is always good, and his goodness is always guiding you. God is good to prepare you. God is good to speak to you. God is good to guide you.

Just as we know, seasons continually blow in and out, and storms will ebb and flow; it's the same for our spiritual seasons and storms. The season will change, and the storm will end, but I encourage you not to miss the goodness of God guiding you. I don't know precisely how God will prepare you for the coming season, but he will. I don't know what word he will give you as an anchor amid the storm, but he has one. Let his Spirit speak to you and remind you that his goodness is guidance.

Chapter Five Reflection

1. Can you identify the present season you are in? How does it compare to the season that came before? And what season do you believe lies ahead?

2. In the present season, is there a storm through which you are wading or that you feel is headed your way? If yes, ask the Holy Spirit to give you a Scripture to cling to as your anchor amid the storm.

3. Take a moment to surrender your present season and ask the Holy Spirit to help your heart and mind be inclined to hear his voice as seasons change and storms arise, allowing God's goodness to be your guide.

six

My Goodness Brings Repentance

The goodness of God to a man of evil life is not intended to encourage him to continue in his sin, but it is meant to woo and win him away from it.

—Charles Spurgeon

ONE DAY WHILE SCROLLING ON PINTEREST, I CAME across a post of funny church signs. So, like most of us, I lost self-control and went down the rabbit hole. I clicked on the funny church sign and then read too many of them to count. I came across a few that were pretty witty and made me chuckle. Then I read a few that left me wide-eyed:

- "Beware of the high cost of low living."
- "Eternity: Smoking or Nonsmoking."
- "100 degrees is cold compared to hell."
- "Stop, drop, and roll doesn't work in hell."

These signs left me with pause. While the play on words is amusing, and there is a bit of truth to the sayings, I felt put off by the signs.

Maybe my degree in public relations caused me to cringe when I read them, but I don't think so. I think my small recoil was for all the actual passersby. I imagine the sayings intended to get the attention of those driving by in hopes of getting them to evaluate their lives. I wonder if the signs did their job?

I have been in many church services where the preacher stands on stage, red-faced, screaming and spitting, preaching the "repent or go to hell" sermon. As a child, these types of sermons scared me. They put a fear of God in me. Not a fear for God, but the kind of panic where I thought I might end up like Lot's wife, a pillar of salt, if I wasn't careful. This forced and scary repentance turned my heart to serve God out of thinking he might strike me down instead of serving him out of love and honor. Attempting to serve God from a fearful mindset caused my heart to misunderstand the heart of God. This misunderstanding ended up leaving me a broken and sinful believer.

God calls us to repentance. He calls us to live a life turned from the ways of the world that would bring us harm and ultimately separate us from him. God calls us to repentance not because he is mean but because of his great love for us. There are many ways to attempt to get the message of repentance out: funny or not-so-funny church signs, screaming preachers, picketing and protesting outside of buildings. Still, there is one way God desires for repentance to be communicated—through goodness. The goodness of God calls us all to repentance, the believer and unbeliever alike. Goodness calls us to repentance, so we can live in relationship with God and fulfill the purpose he has for us.

Good Harlot

Joshua just received the honor and commission to lead the Israelites out of the wilderness and into their promise. The promise was flowing with milk and honey but was also overtaken by

My Goodness Brings Repentance

all the *-ites*. The first place the Israelites were to conquer was the city of Jericho. Like a good leader, Joshua wanted to know what lay ahead of them. So he sent two spies into the city to do a little scouting work. While the spies were in Jericho, they came across Rahab, a harlot, and lodged at her house. There were probably a few reasons why they chose her home. One, it was located inside the wall of the city, which made it easier to come in and out. Two, she was a harlot, meaning men would go in and out, men from the city and visitors. A high-traffic home made the spies less visible. Word got around that some men from the Israelite camp were in the town. So the king sent word to Rahab, asking her if those men had come to her. She said, "Yes, the men did come to me, but I didn't know where they were from" (Josh. 2:4). She took the two Israelite spies and hid them on her roof.

After the king's men left, she asked the men she hid to treat her and her father's house kindly when they returned to take the city. And they agreed. She helped the men escape from the city, and then she waited. I don't know how Rahab found herself to be a harlot. But I can guarantee you, she didn't dream of being a harlot when she was a little girl. But somehow, through some unfortunate circumstances, a harlot was what she had become. So, when the knock came at her door, and two unknown men stood before her, I can imagine she assumed they wanted from her what every other man wanted from her. But instead of being used for sex, she was used for security. I imagine the opportunity to be used for good was one she wouldn't want to pass up.

She, like the other people in the city, was aware of what God had done for the Israelites to bring them out of Egypt. Remember, their hearts were all melting in fear. But Rahab, even in her difficult life, allowed the goodness of God, through men, to turn her heart toward repentance. We see this in her actions to help hide and cover up the spies. She could have embraced her common way of life and trusted in the men of the city who enjoyed her trade. Or she could risk it all and turn from her sin and embrace the God of Israel, embrace the chance at a real relationship. I imagine deep down, she wanted out of the lifestyle in which she lived. But nothing seemed to change—until one day, when goodness came knocking on her door, wanting to use her for a bigger purpose.

She surely heard the sound of them coming. The Israelites showed up and started marching around the city for seven days. Then the walls came tumbling down. The spies, now warriors, entered the city and rescued Rahab and her family. The goodness of God extended to Rahab, the harlot, in her sin, amid her messy life, and she found repentance. Rahab went on to marry Salmon and gave birth to Boaz. And if you follow that lineage, you will end up at Jesus. The goodness of God reached down to Rahab, the harlot. It called her to repentance. It drew her into relationship. It set her up with purpose to be in the lineage of our Absolute Goodness (Josh. 2–6).

Rahab wasn't an Israelite; she wasn't a daughter of Abraham. She was a harlot, an outsider; and even in all that, goodness found her in the wall of a city and led her to repentance. We are all like Rahab at some point in our lives. We have all been outsiders to the family of God. But God met me while I was hiding in the walls of my world, extended his goodness, and turned my rebel heart into a heart of repentance. The goodness of God has the power to break down any walls we have and reach our hearts. His goodness finds us in our broken world, in our mess, and reaches down and gently guides us into his family through repentance, propelling us into purpose.

Here's the truth: even after my heart turned toward repentance, I found myself not a sinner needing grace and mercy, but a believer still needing to repent. Repentance isn't a one-time thing. Initially, when we become believers, yes, we do make a radical change, a

180-degree turn. We have headed one direction, but now we do a dramatic turnaround, all thanks to the goodness of God. But even as we are moving in the right direction in our relationship with God, we must recognize that we still need a heart of repentance, a heart willing to allow the goodness of God to guide our heart continually in a right relationship with him.

Good Fish

The word "repentance," or "repent," can be a word we tend to shy away from. We don't like words that make us feel uncomfortable or that might make others feel uneasy. Unfortunately, this word has received a bad rap and now lives in the column of negative words in our world. The word "repent" is repeated throughout the Bible, and Jesus said, "Repent, for the kingdom of heaven is at hand" (Matt. 4:17 ESV). But now when we are in church, screaming preacher or not, and we hear the word "repent," the pew sitters grow uneasy. Repentance is designed to draw us into a relationship with God, not drive us into rebellion. Sadly, the enemy has weaseled his way into the concept of repentance. So when called to repent, we want to dig our boots in the ground and stay our course in rebellion. But if we allow our minds to see repentance as access to relationship, then we shift the concept from being a negative one to one of hope. This is done only through goodness, but goodness comes in pretty unique ways.

    The same goodness that created the world, that created you and me, draws us to his heart. But to access the fullness of God, we must seek repentance. The story of Jonah is quite a fascinating story. God called Jonah to go to Nineveh and call out to her people because of their evil behavior. Jonah didn't want to be the messenger of repentance, so he turned to rebellion and ran. He wasn't even the one being asked to repent; yet somehow, he was the one running in the opposite direction. There might be times when God wants to use you and me to express his goodness, leading others to repentance, but we must be careful not to let it drive us to rebellion; we must instead allow it to press us into our relationship with him, drawing others to him.

Jonah continued to run, jumped on a boat, and set sail. While on the craft, Jonah took a peaceful nap while everyone else freaked out because of a raging storm. They awoke Jonah, he admitted this entire situation was his fault, and, after some convincing, they threw him overboard. The Scripture says a great fish swallowed Jonah, and he sat in the belly of the fish for three days and three nights. But there in the stomach of the fish, Jonah found himself seeking repentance. I don't know many of us who would think that being swallowed by a giant fish was good, but if the goodness of God leads to repentance, that makes being gulped up by a fish God's goodness. Sometimes the goodness of God comes in the strangest ways. We must be willing to see and receive goodness even if we are in the belly of a fish.

Sitting in the sloshing stomach, Jonah cried out to God, seeking repentance. Then that fish spat Jonah out. God once again spoke to Jonah, telling him to go to Nineveh and call the people to repentance. Jonah, having sought repentance for himself, then conceded to be used for a purpose by God. Jonah reached Nineveh and proclaimed a short message: "Another forty days and Nineveh will be overthrown!" (Jon. 3:4). And God in his goodness, through a reluctant messenger, called the city to repentance, and the people did. God saw the repentant hearts of the Ninevites, and he relented from their punishment. The goodness of God was sent through a messenger to a town to call them to repentance. Nineveh didn't let the message of repentance cause their hearts to rebel, but instead, they saw the goodness of God and allowed repentance to fix their relationship.

Jonah, the prophet, a man of God, who sought repentance for himself, brought the goodness of repentance to a city, but found himself struggling with the goodness of God. That same goodness that led him to repentance is the same goodness that led the city of Nineveh to turn from their sin. Yet Jonah found himself in a fit of anger with God over goodness. Jonah felt angry enough to die—he must've really had something against Nineveh. God, in his great goodness, continued to engage with Jonah, offering opportunities for his heart to embrace the goodness of repentance—even for his foe. Jonah 4 ends with a question from God for Jonah: "You have pity on the plant for which you did no labor or make it grow, that appeared overnight and perished overnight. So shouldn't I have pity on Nineveh—the great city that has in it more than 120,000 people who don't know their right hand from their left—as well as many animals?" (Jon. 4:10). We don't know Jonah's response to God, but we can see the goodness of God offering Jonah the opportunity to embrace the repentance that he offers to all of his creation. Jonah the prophet needed the goodness of God to lead him to repentance. We need the goodness of God to lead us to repentance. But we have a choice to accept the goodness that is offered before us. Nineveh had a choice. Jonah had a choice. You and I have the choice to choose the goodness of repentance. We must be willing to hear the goodness of God in the cry of repentance, and we must be ready to be used to offer the goodness of God, drawing others to repentance.

Good Women

Jesus demonstrates goodness that leads to repentance throughout the Gospels. As he encounters person after person, as goodness now personified, he continually drew the hearts of people into a relationship with the Father. Jesus was willing to meet anyone, anywhere. He extended goodness no matter where they were in the faith, believer or not, or somewhere in between.

Samaritan

We see this in action as he sat at a well in Samaria and encountered a woman. A Samaritan woman, to be exact—meaning she acted Jewish when it benefited her and lived a pagan life other times.[1] Society and customs said Jesus shouldn't have been anywhere close to her and her mixed-up life and ideas. But goodness wants to meet even someone whose life is a disaster and whose form of faith is not quite right.

As believers, we often have a form of faith, one taught to us, one that we believe in, but we are still far from where we should be. We live out our faith the best we know how or how we feel is best for us, but we have yet to encounter the goodness of repentance intimately. Even as believers, we must allow our hearts to be open to the goodness of repentance, allowing our lives to be forever changed.

John writes of this incredible encounter of goodness when Jesus met this Samaritan woman at the well, offering her a new life. Jesus and his disciples traveled from Judea to Galilee and went through Samaria. While the disciples walked to the town to buy food, Jesus, alone and exhausted, sat by the well. It was around midday when a woman approached the well. It was a little late in the day to be drawing water, but this woman was coming for water in the afternoon, and Jesus asked for a drink. This request caught the Samaritan woman off guard. Jesus, a Jew, and she, a Samaritan woman, shouldn't have been talking, shouldn't have been alone, shouldn't be sharing water.

She felt hesitant to give him water, but Jesus told her if she only knew who was asking for a drink, she would have asked him for a drink instead. Jesus told her about living water, about the water that would cause her never to thirst again. And, of course, she wants some of that water. Water that would keep her from traveling to the well at noon, trying to lessen the shame of her life. Water that would free her from going back and forth to the well, perhaps overhearing the whispers about her. Yes, she wanted that water! Any water that good, I would want too.

But then Jesus told her to go call her husband. And I'm sure the shame she thought would disappear started to rise again as she told him she didn't have a husband. Jesus agreed with her, and then said she had had five husbands and was now living with a man who was not her husband. The woman realized he was a prophet and found herself confused by their different beliefs. And then Jesus brought it home; he told her of true salvation, of worshiping in Spirit and truth, and corrected what she had always believed. She then claimed to know that Messiah and to know that he was coming. "Then Jesus declared, 'I, the one speaking to you—I am he'" (John 4:26 NIV).

The Samaritan woman, the woman who thought she believed in what was right, the woman who lived how she wanted, had just encountered the goodness of God. It told her the things she had done wrong but didn't shame her; instead, it invited her to live a life better than before. The woman then ran back to her town to tell everyone of the goodness of God. The goodness that led her to repentance offered true salvation. It set her on a path of purpose, offering the same goodness to the town around her.

Adulteress

Here's another significant story of Jesus, of goodness, leading to repentance in the book of John. Jesus began to teach in the temple when the scribes and Pharisees disrupted the scene. They dragged in a woman caught in adultery. They put her in the middle of the crowd and asked Jesus what he thought should happen to her. Unfortunately, this poor woman found in the middle of a manipulation scheme was now in the middle of the temple. People crowded around her, she stood in all of her sins, and I imagine shame flushed her face. The Pharisees wanted her stoned, per the Torah. They wanted her sin exposed; they wanted Jesus trapped. They wanted zero goodness involved and no room for repentance.

Jesus gently bent down and started writing in the dirt. Scripture doesn't tell us what he wrote, but he wrote something significant then simply asked if there were any among them who were without sin. If so, then they could throw a stone at her. Then he started to write in the dirt again, and one by one, oldest to youngest, the people began to fade away.

Now alone in the temple with the adulteress woman, "Jesus straightened up and asked her, 'Woman, where are they? Has no one condemned you?' 'No one, sir,' she said. 'Then neither do I condemn you,' Jesus declared. 'Go now and leave your life of sin'" (John 8:10–11 NIV).

The goodness of God calls us to repentance but not through shameful exposure like the Pharisees had intended. When sin is shamefully exposed, and then repentance is called for, we are left with hurt and tempted to have a heart of rebellion. But when sin is revealed without condemnation but through the goodness of God, repentance draws our hearts into relationship.

Jesus was very clear when he told this woman not to sin anymore, calling her to an act of repentance. But that calling to repentance was done through the love of goodness. We must allow the goodness of God to continually reveal the sin in our lives, leading us to repentance. And we must be cautious to not expose the sins of others through shame and condemnation, but instead allow the goodness of God to flow through us, drawing hearts to repentance and into right relationship with our Father.

Good Girl

One day, I experienced the goodness of repentance through the love of goodness. It happened as I sat in the pews of the church I grew up in. I was home from college for the summer and in a relationship that I knew I should leave. I knew this wasn't the person I was going to marry, but I couldn't leave the relationship. I should have been moving on, but I continued to cling to something I knew God was calling me away from. I needed to turn from the relationship; I needed to repent for my disobedience, but I didn't. On this particular Sunday morning, while I was living in direct opposition to God's will, I encountered the goodness that led me to repentance.

I stood and sang all the songs then sat in the pew that morning service like I did most of my life. There happened to be a guest speaker that morning, someone I had never met in my life, and still to this day, I have no idea what his name is. He preached his sermon, and I don't remember what he taught. But then he opened the altars for prayer and offered to pray with and for anyone who wanted prayer. I continued to reverently sit in my seat while others went to the front to pray. The next thing I knew, the preacher said, "YOU," and was looking and pointing directly at me. My face became red and flushed, and I slowly stood up to head to the front to see what he wanted to say to me. Honestly, I thought I was going to break out in a full sweat. I was so nervous the man was going to call my sin out in front of everyone. But I continued to walk to the front of the church until I stood face-to-face with the evangelist.

While standing in front of this man who didn't know me, and whom I didn't know, he began to speak what the Lord had spoken to his heart for me. He said, "Your husband is on his way. You will know him by his love to serve the Lord. Together, you will have a ministry that will lead thousands to the Lord." I stood there in my sin of disobedience with tears streaming down my face. All the while, the goodness of God spoke to my future, to my purpose, leading my heart to repentance.

That relationship ended, and I returned to school in the fall, where I met my wonderful husband, Brad. The goodness of God led me to repentance. It wasn't condemnation and shame of my sin that changed my heart but goodness that led my heart to repentance.

Good Saul

Saul of Tarsus became Paul on the road to Damascus through the goodness of God. Saul, born in Tarsus, was Jewish but also had the much-desired Roman citizenship. Saul studied the Hebrew Scriptures under the famous rabbi Gamaliel. He lived in the best of all the worlds, from citizenship to education. Saul believed so strongly in what he learned that he started persecuting those who believed in the Messiah. Saul was a believer in the Law; he thought what he was doing was right and for a good cause. Even in his belief, he was a sinner in need of goodness. He needed an encounter with goodness to turn his heart toward repentance and into a relationship.

Saul was so zealous that he missed the mark and needed something more significant. As believers, we must be careful that we don't find ourselves sinful in a fight for what is right and wrong—so stiff that we miss the mark of relationship. Saul persecuted Christians and even approved the stoning of Stephen. Saul was responsible for the imprisonment of Christ-followers. Saul, the educated Jewish scholar and zealot, was in desperate need of repentance.

Saul, traveling the road to Damascus on his way to arrest Christians, was taken by surprise. A light from heaven flashed around him, and then he heard a voice. I don't know which is wilder: a giant fish swallowing Jonah or bright lights and an unknown voice! Saul fell on the ground, which begins a conversation:

> Then he fell to the ground, and heard a voice saying to him, "Saul, Saul, why are you persecuting Me?"
> And he said, "Who are You, Lord?
> Then the Lord said, "I am Jesus, whom you are persecuting. It is hard for you to kick against the goads."
> So he, trembling and astonished, said, "Lord, what do You want me to do?"
> Then the Lord said to him, "Arise and go into the city, and you will be told what you must do." (Acts 9:4–6 NKJV)

Saul, now blind, was led to Damascus, where he had a divine encounter. Ananias received word from the Lord to meet Saul, speak to him, and pray for him. Ananias, a bit hesitant having known the kind of man Saul was, went on in obedience. He entered into the house where Saul waited and said,

> "Brother Saul, the Lord Jesus, who appeared to you on the road as you came, has sent me that you may receive your sight and be filled with the Holy Spirit." Immediately there fell from his eyes something like scales, and he received his sight at once; and he arose and was baptized. (Acts 9:17–18 NKJV)

After his baptism, Saul ate and spent time with the disciples, then immediately began proclaiming the name of Jesus. Saul, a man who thought he knew the way, found himself in desperate need of repentance, and goodness led him there.

Goodness showed up as a bright light and an audible voice, grabbing Saul by the heart and leading him to repentance, restoring relationship, giving him a new name and a new purpose. Goodness showed up through a faithful servant willing to speak love and truth.

Embrace Goodness

Whether it's a knock at the door of your home, in the belly of a fish, in the middle of a church service, or through a bright light, we must let our hearts be inclined to allow the goodness of God to lead us to repentance and resist the enemy's push to vilify it. The enemy wants to take the idea of repentance and twist it in our minds because he knows that without repentance, there is a separation in our relationship with the Father. The enemy wants to take moments in our lives and distort them, causing us to have a skewed vision of goodness. But we must be aware that goodness is continually working, even in the most unusual moments. It's the goodness of God that leads us to repentance, leading us into right relationship, and relationship propels us into purpose.

My prayer is that our hearts be receptive to the goodness that leads to repentance no matter what it looks like. May our hearts be sensitive and ready to turn from or give up whatever may be causing distance in our relationship with our Father. And may we act as vessels willing to be used to extend the goodness of God to the world around us. May we forever let our lives reflect the goodness of God so that those around us will be drawn into repentance, into a relationship with the good Father.

Chapter Six Reflection

1. What are your feelings toward the word or concept of *repentance*? Are you accepting of the idea that Jesus calls us to repentance or are you a bit jaded to the concept? Why do you feel one way or another about repentance?

2. Take a moment and ask the Holy Spirit to reveal anything in your life that might be causing distance in your relationship

with the Father. (Maybe it's a lie you are believing, a behavior you are participating in, or an act of obedience you are shying away from.)

3. Now take a prayerful moment and repent, asking forgiveness and asking for the Holy Spirit to help you continue to walk away from that former sin and walk boldly in relationship with the Father.

Note

[1] Flavius Josephus, *The Complete Works Josephus*, trans. William Whiston (Nashville: Thomas Nelson, 1998), 316–17.

seven

My Goodness Is an Experience

*A saint is not someone who is good
but who experiences the goodness of God.*

—Brennan Manning

When we read the Scripture "Taste and see that the Lord is good" (Ps. 34:8 NIV), it can create a puzzle in our minds. We may not consciously evaluate the tension, but we do it subconsciously. We brush Scripture like this under the metaphorical rug and move onto the next Scripture. We quote it in situations that seem appropriate but fall short when trying to reconcile how to taste and see the very physical goodness, which is far from tangible. So instead of embracing the reality of tasting and seeing goodness, we tuck it in our pocket to make us feel good. But pulling out Scripture in tough moments to make you feel good will leave you feeling less than good. Yes, Scripture can make you feel good and bring joy into the pain. But there are moments in this life, tough ones, when just saying a Scripture doesn't suffice. You need that Scripture to move from metaphorical to reality. There are moments when we need more than just to believe and quote "taste and see," but we need actually to taste and see that God is good.

Taste

My mom has always been a fantastic cook. I firmly believe it is a gift God gave her. When my mom was young, my grandmother worked multiple jobs; it became my mom's responsibility to cook and clean the house and care for her little sister. A lot of times, there wasn't much in the cabinets or refrigerator, yet she was always able to create a wonderful meal for her family. That gift carried over as she married and started her family. I always say she can make meat out of flour. She can turn the simplest of ingredients into the best southern home-cooked meal.

Unfortunately, I didn't get this gift. As a child, I spent most of my time watching the Cowboys or Bulls play with my brother and dad, and during the commercial breaks, I would go clean up after her or set the table. So now, as a mother and wife, I struggle every night at dinnertime with my family. Food is always on the table—sometimes it tastes good, and other times it turns into frozen pizza night. God gave us the ability to taste and smell what is good or bad; the two go hand in hand. We get to eat of the fine foods he placed on this earth. We get to taste the food from the creative hands of chefs. We have the opportunity to indulge in the savory and sweet pleasures of food. Our ability to taste and smell gives us the ability to perceive what tastes good or bad.

See

I started wearing glasses when I was in first grade. I was farsighted, meaning I couldn't see things up close. My first pair of glasses was quite cute (insert sarcasm). The frames were almost transparent at the top of the circle and then faded down to pink at the bottom. The lenses were as round and thick as a tennis ball—or at least that's how my first-grade mind remembers them. Over time, my eyes moved along the scale, and a couple of years later, I was no longer farsighted but was suddenly nearsighted and couldn't see far away. The good news was I could get a new pair of really cool spectacles. Thin gold and brown frames with flat lenses circled my chocolate brown eyes, and I felt good. My struggle to see as a kid was a problem. I couldn't see near; then I couldn't see far. Seeing was something I was used to, and when I couldn't see like before, it was time to evaluate my problem. God gave us vision so that we can see the colors in their vast array spread across the earth and the canvas of the universe. Our ability to see gives us the capability to perceive what is good or bad around us, to experience the goodness of God.

Taste and vision are part of the five senses God gave us to enjoy this life. Both of these senses allow us to perceive and experience the goodness of God. But when one of our functioning senses starts to diminish, we begin to lose our ability to discern correctly. Suddenly, the good and bad start to mix, and it is hard to tell the difference between the two. Like when we burn our tongue, and then our ability to taste is off. Or if we get poked in the eye, then we can't see clearly. Our senses are out of whack and cause us not to taste and see correctly—so it is when sudden moments of life strike hard. For a moment our senses can become damaged, causing us not to perceive what is good from the bad. It is the heart of the Father for us to taste and see his goodness, to experience it. But we have to allow our vision to be cleared and taste to be adjusted—all our senses to be heightened—so we can experience the goodness of God in the land of the living (Ps. 27:13).

Daily Goodness

The Hebrew people saw goodness through the many perils God sent to set them free from Egypt. They must have smelled goodness, though it came in the stench of death around them (Exod. 7–12). And they tasted goodness as they ate the Passover lamb. Their senses where awakened to the goodness of God as they pressed their way toward their promise. While wandering in the wilderness in pursuit of the promise, God continued to awaken their senses, allowing them to experience his never-ending goodness.

Goodness was continually on display for them to taste and see. As the children of Israel roamed, they were thirsty, hungry, and angry. A combination called *hangry*. Yet, God, in his infinite goodness, provided. Through meeting the physical needs of his children, God put his goodness on display not just so they could taste and see, but also so they could engage and experience.

Following their miraculous crossing of the Sea of Reeds, the Israelites encountered their first wilderness moment of thirst; and God was ready to meet their need. The children of God stopped at Marah, where there was water but water they couldn't drink. This stream before them was bitter and unable to meet their need. But God wanted his children to know his goodness was with them every step of the way. So even when it seemed their need wouldn't be met, God was going to allow them to experience his goodness. Moses cried out to God for an answer, and the Lord showed him a tree. Moses threw the tree into the water, and the water turned sweet. Moses allowed his eyes to be opened to see the goodness of God, illuminated to see what God wanted him to see: the tree. When the tree splashed into the stream, bitterness turned to sweetness. When we see the goodness of God, it turns even the most bitter moments into sweet goodness for us to taste. There at Marah, the Israelites saw, they tasted, and they experienced the goodness of God (Exod. 15).

As they moved on from Marah, they experienced quail covering the camp. And mornings where manna, white like coriander seed and tasting like sweet honey, appeared as frost on the ground. They could now taste, see, and experience goodness every day, meeting their every need (Exod. 16–17).

And as they continued their journey, they saw goodness go before and behind them. Goodness rose steadily before their eyes as they began to sacrifice. The number of animals called to be sacrificed, the amount of food to be offered, was significant, yet the goodness of God always provided. They could see the goodness of God in their provision. And as the priests would butcher the animals, sprinkle the red blood, and set fire on the altar, the goodness of God was ever visible to the Israelites. And as the aroma of the sacrifices rose to the heavens in a pillar of smoke, so the smell of the goodness reached out and touched the mouths of God's children. They could taste and see the goodness of God.

The Israelites continually experienced the goodness of God through the sacrifices of atonement that brought them into right relationship with God. We, too, can experience the goodness of God in our daily lives. Every day, we are called to offer ourselves as a living sacrifice, to die to self, and as we do that, we experience the goodness of God. It is essential to experience goodness daily because there will be days it will be harder to find. Goodness is readily available for us to taste and see, but life sometimes sends a fog blocking our senses.

Present Goodness

Job experienced what was probably one of the most gut-wrenching tragedies this world will ever read about. One day, Job's life was full—full of family, animals, friends, and security. Then, in an instant, it was all turned upside down. One by one, servants entered Job's home and delivered blow after blow of heart-aching news. This news left him undone, naked, with his head shaved, and on the ground in worship. Job handled this life-altering event better than just about any human could. The Scripture tells us he didn't sin or cast reproach on God during this process. But it did leave him grieving, in pain, full of questions, and stuck.

We all experience tragedy and grief in some way during our lives. We experience it differently, handle it a bit differently, but a few things remain the same: we will have questions, and we will all feel stuck in that moment. I am sure Job didn't know how his life would ever move past the new reality staring him in the face. He was stuck in his grief with questions. Even though days counted on, Job was unable to move in that moment of pain. This happens to us too; but more often than not, it's not just days or even months, but years and decades that pass. We try to move on, but our minds, reactions, and questions are all still stuck in a single moment that left us with pause and left our senses blocked from experiencing full goodness.

Job, there in his grief, didn't sin but did ask questions. I wish I could say the same for myself. When I found myself stuck in a moment, decades past the actual moment, I had done the opposite of Job. I sinned in my grief and never asked any questions. The sin separated, put a distance between, goodness and myself, causing me to miss it altogether. But Job didn't sin; he just had an earnest heart-to-heart with God.

This vapor of time in Job's life must have felt like an eternity. And by all accounts, it appeared as if the goodness of God had ceased for the day. Job even says, "My days are swifter than a runner; they flee away without seeing goodness" (Job 9:25). In the standstill of pain, Job knew his days were quickly passing, and he could see no good before him. Goodness was blurred by the miseries of life, making it hard for him to taste and see the goodness of God. The moments that shake us to our very core, the moments like Job's, when life will forever be a bit different, cause us to believe we can't see the good.

The enemy asked for permission to afflict Job, and God allowed it. In an attempt to get Job to turn away from his faith, the enemy tried to distort the goodness of God. But in the moment, Job pressed on, even in the grief when he couldn't see goodness, and poured his heart out. When we face the trials of this life, the enemy will be there in full force, attempting to distort the goodness of God, trying to drive a wedge in our relationship with God. It's so hard to see goodness when our world feels shattered.

But even through blurred vision, Job fixed his eyes and said, "I had heard of You by the hearing of the ear; but now my eye has seen You" (Job 42:5). Job saw the goodness of God even in the midst of tragedy. Job didn't try to put on his strong face and act like all was well. He fell to the ground, the only secure thing in his life, and sought the Father. It took a little time, but Job saw the goodness of God in his grief. Job moved from just hearing about God and his goodness to seeing goodness with his own eyes. It is God's desire for us to experience him continually, but life has a way of distorting our senses. But God, in the middle of our mess, still wants to meet us there. Life has a way of turning out different than we hope or expect. It's those moments that cause us to question God, to question goodness.

Past Goodness

One moment can forever change the trajectory of our lives. In an instant, what we once knew is now marked by a moment of pain, abuse, tragedy, divorce, abandonment, and countless others. As time moves on, physically, so do we, but often emotionally, we stay stuck in that life-changing moment. From then on, the way we see ourselves, the way we see God, the way we think and view life now filters through the lens of that one moment. Most of us do this subconsciously, never realizing the filters we have put in place that alter the way we experience God.

In the Gospel of Luke, there is a compelling story about a sinful woman who washed Jesus's feet. Jesus was a guest in the house of a Pharisee. There he sat at the table to enjoy a meal. The sinful woman heard Jesus would be at this house, and she went to find him. The Scripture tells us this woman was a sinner, and she owned an expensive bottle of perfume. It would be reasonable to gather she was a prostitute. Her perfume was worth a great deal of money. It was her security. It's what proved how good she was at her job. But like Rahab, like the woman at the well, this woman was desperate to find a way out of her present life. But life happens and marks us, and our lives are forever changed; her life was now marked. If this woman was ever going to be free from her life, from the moment that changed her, she had to experience goodness. Finding goodness in the pain of life was vital for this woman's freedom, and it is for ours, too.

This sinful woman found herself as someone she didn't want to be and was desperate to be free. She didn't care what people thought. She didn't care who saw; she just wanted to be free. So she crashed the party. She sat somewhere she wasn't authorized to sit. She did something people didn't like, all in her desperation to find Jesus, to find goodness so that she could be free. As she let herself into the house filled with the special guests of the Pharisee all sitting around the table, she made her way to him.

She, like Job, found her way to the ground where Jesus's feet rested. And there she wept; I'm sure a hush came over the room. All eyes fixed on the sin kneeling and crying at the feet of the guest of honor. Her tears began to drip, then to pour over Jesus's feet. All the years of pain and hurt surrendered in warm streams from her face to his feet. The woman uncovered her hair and let it fall down, as she must have done so many times before with men. But as she dried his feet with her hair, she surrendered herself to her Savior.

I can imagine mouths were gaping open in shock of her actions and the lack of Jesus's. And finally, she took her prized possession from around her neck and poured the perfume on his feet. She had now surrendered any security she had in this world. The aroma of her perfume filled the air, like the aroma of the sacrifices offered by the Israelites, reaching heaven. The scent of her sacrifice, so strong you could taste it, touched the heart of Jesus and overwhelmed those watching.

The host grew angry and wanted answers. And Jesus gave him some. But more importantly, he forgave the woman. "Then He said to her, 'Your sins are forgiven.' And those who sat at the table with Him began to say to themselves, 'Who is this who even forgives sins?' Then He said to the woman, 'Your faith has saved you. Go in peace'" (Luke 7:48–50 NKJV).

She went looking for Jesus, goodness, the only one who could bring healing to her past and peace to her future, and she found him. She was no longer bound by the hurt of her past, the choices she had made, or a future of fear because she saw goodness with her own eyes. She perceived he was good, so she went and experienced his goodness. Goodness was on display for all to taste and see that day, for all to experience. Goodness is in every moment of our lives, even the worst ones. We must be willing to find it and experience it.

God was, is, and is to come, which means it doesn't matter if we are like Job, seeking goodness right in the moment, or like this woman, seeking goodness for her past hurts and present forgiveness; God will reveal his goodness. Past or present, if we seek him, we will find him; he will show us hidden things (Jer. 33:3; Matt. 7:7). His goodness, though it feels concealed at times, will be revealed through the illumination of the Holy Spirit, bringing healing to the painful moments and allowing us to move forward in complete freedom.

Not Forsaken

Jesus died on the cross so that we could experience, so we could taste and see, his goodness by living forgiven and free. That means freedom from our sin and freedom from being stuck. But before Jesus went to the cross, he sat and ate with his disciples. They partook of the Passover meal and reflected on their forefathers and the great acts God did to deliver the Israelites. The idea of freedom resonated with their hearts. The concept of goodness being something to experience was one they must have understood. But there, Jesus sat ready to settle goodness once and for all. He broke the freshly baked bread and said, "Take, eat; this is My body" (Matt. 26:26). And the ruby-colored wine was poured, and he said, "Drink from it, all of you" (Matt. 26:27).

Jesus then took our place on the cross as atonement for our sins. But as Jesus hung there, "And about the ninth hour Jesus cried out with a loud voice, saying, 'Eli, Eli, lama sabachthani?' that is, 'My God, my God, why have you forsaken Me?'" (Matt. 27:46 ESV). Jesus cried out in all of his humanity, feeling the weight of the world, and wondered where his father was. David experienced moments like this. Job must have wondered this. The sinful woman surely wondered where God was in her pain. We have all experienced moments like this, where it feels like God has forsaken us.

Maybe it was in abuse, infidelity, infertility, or tragedy. The list could go on and on of opportunities for us to feel like, for a brief moment in time, God has forsaken us. Jesus felt that same feeling we feel. He knows all too well the chasm that feeling can create. In that moment of feeling abandoned, that's when we get stuck, that's when goodness gets blurred. But let me assure you, God did not forsake his son on the cross. God did not even for a moment forsake David, Job, the sinful woman, or you and me. He says in his Word, "He will not leave you or forsake you" (Deut. 31:6 ESV). He doesn't turn his back on us. He doesn't look away. He never forsakes us. That means in that painful moment, he was still there. And if you missed him there, if you missed his goodness, you can always find it now. His goodness is available for us to taste and see, for us to experience. Not just right now but in our past too. Goodness is readily available for us to taste and see.

Experiencing goodness in our past can seem a bit odd. People often say, don't look back; you're not going that way. No, we don't want to go backward; we all want to move forward. But sometimes the only way to move forward is to go back. Going back to the moment that emotionally took us captive and distorted the goodness of God is the only way to move forward in complete freedom. When we allow our hearts and minds to return to the past while the Holy Spirit is guiding us, then we can experience the goodness of God in our past.

Asking the Holy Spirit to guide us back to the painful moments isn't easy. Trying to see the goodness of God in moments when all we saw was hurt feels risky and uncertain. But there is no moment in our lives that the Holy Spirit is scared of. God wasn't frightened by his son's death, and he didn't forsake him. He brought forth ultimate goodness. And God wants to reveal his goodness in the moments when you may have felt abandoned.

A couple of years ago, I was talking to one of my most trusted mentors on this earth. She is older than I and is a warrior of the faith. In her young childhood, she was molested by a family member. She made many poor choices as so many do following the pain of violation, but she found her way to her Savior. She made the choice to allow the Holy Spirit to bring healing, restoration, and forgiveness. But as we talked on the phone that day, I asked her a very tough question. I asked, "Where do you think

God was when your family member did this to you?" She paused and replied, "I don't think he left me. I just think he must have turned his back."

Wait a minute! This woman of God, a pillar of faith, thought God had turned his back on her in her most painful moment. This woman who had overcome so much through the power of the Holy Spirit still believed God looked away in her darkest moment. Let me tell you: there is no moment, no pain, nothing that God has to turn away from. He is God, and while he detests sin, he can handle whatever we have gone through or are going through.

I replied to her calmly, "I don't think there is anything that God is scared of or has to turn away from. But why don't you ask him? Ask the Holy Spirit to reveal where he was in that painful moment. It won't be easy, because no one wants to dwell on the hurt that reshapes her, but I can promise you God will show up." A couple of weeks later, while talking on the phone again, she said, "I asked what you told me to ask." And I replied, "What did he reveal?" She was almost afraid to give her answer, because she didn't want it to be weird. But she finally told me what the Holy Spirit revealed about the presence of God in that past moment.

God illuminated his presence in her painful past. He opened her eyes to see he never left, he never looked away, he was with her. This allowed her to experience, to see, goodness in the worst moments of her life. She had to decide to ask the Holy Spirit to reveal goodness in the dark moments of her life. I have done the same, and I encourage you to as well. I can assure you, if you ask, you will receive. He will show you hidden things. God desires to reveal himself to you, even in the worst moments, because if we can find and experience the goodness of God there, then we can live a life of freedom. Wilfrid Stinissen said this:

As soon as you show him [God] your wounds and expose yourself to his healing power, the healing process begins, one that is not like ordinary healing. It is not a question of something old that has caused you much pain and finally ceases to torment you. The healing goes back into time and transforms the very moment when you were hurt into a moment of grace. The very wound that was the cause of so much suffering is transformed into a blessing, and all the bitterness it caused is changed into meaningful and fruitful suffering.[1]

God wants to turn that moment of pain into a revelation of his goodness. But when we miss goodness, we become vulnerable to the lies the enemy is shooting our way. He preys on our pain and attempts to distort goodness. But we have the power to overcome through the blood of Jesus, to find freedom and experience goodness amid the pain.

- As the Israelites wandered through the dusty wilderness, they could taste and see the goodness of God daily through the provision and act of sacrifice.
- Job, having fallen to the ground and breathing in the dusty earth in all of his grief, saw the goodness of God in the midst of tragedy.
- While perfume was poured on Jesus's feet, the aroma of goodness filled the air.
- Jesus, wearing the weight of every dusty human, feeling forsaken and yet experiencing the closest moment to his Father, ushered in goodness for the entire world.

When we surrender and find ourselves broken on the dusty ground, the Holy Spirit will reveal goodness for us to taste and see. Goodness for us to experience. Taste and see that the Lord is good. The goodness of God is available for us to experience, bringing healing to our lives, offering us a life of complete restoration and freedom.

Chapter Seven Reflection

1. Have you ever felt like there was a moment when God has forsaken you or maybe looked away from you? If you are unsure, take a moment and ask the Holy Spirit to reveal to you any moment when you felt forsaken or any moment in which you believed a lie about the goodness of God.

2. If a memory or moment came to mind, surrender that moment and ask the Holy Spirit to reveal where he was in that memory, and allow your heart to see the goodness of God.

Note

[1] Wilfrid Stinissen, *Into Your Hands, Father: Abandoning Ourselves to the God Who Loves Us*, trans. Clare Marie (San Francisco: Ignatius Press, 2011), 41–42.

eight

My Goodness Is a Seed

The Christian does not think God will love us because we are good, but that God will make us good because He loves us.

—C. S. Lewis

ONE WARM SPRING AFTERNOON, BRAD AND I VISited a home improvement store with our youngest son in tow. As we passed all the beautiful flowers in the outdoor department, Harrison, just four at the time, saw a rack where seed packets hung. Adamant, as most preschoolers are when they want something, we let him pick out a few packets of seeds to plant in our backyard. He picked pumpkins, corn, squash, carrots, and cucumbers. I'll be honest; it took a lot of self-control not to swoop in and tell him what he should pick. I thought, *Corn, really? How in the world will we grow corn in our backyard?* But I let him choose what he wanted. Then we went over and loaded a few bags of soil into our cart, checked out, and headed home.

Once we arrived home, Brad sectioned off a small area in our backyard and made a garden area. We then tilled the ground a bit and filled the new garden with fresh soil. Harrison and I then dug holes and planted seeds in the dark earth and covered them up. Over the next several weeks, we watered the black soil and waited. Harrison went outside every day, waiting for something to break forth from the ground. Then, at last, something green broke through the soil. Over the next couple of months, we watched the tiny green stem grow into beautiful vines with glowing buds. The corn soon sprouted up and became as tall as Harrison. A few of the other seeds planted in the darkness of the soil broke through full of life and color.

Our lives aren't that different. We are but just a seed planted in the depths of the womb, woven together with purpose, breaking forth in full color on display for the world to see. As God knitted each one of us together, he did so with the fabric of who he is. Every person, you and me, was created in his image, giving us the title of sons and daughters, image-bearers. With goodness being at the very core of God, Jesus (our Absolute Goodness), and the Holy Spirit (the revealer of goodness), being made in their image places the seed of goodness in our hearts.

Image

"Then God said, 'Let Us make man in Our image, after Our likeness! . . .' God created humankind in His image, in the image of God He created him, male and female He created them" (Gen. 1:26–27). The Trinity made male and female in their image to reflect their nature. Each one of us was knit together from the heart of God: "For you created my inmost being; you knit me together in my mother's womb" (Ps. 139:13 NIV). God's spirit, being good, formed man and woman and sealed them with his words of goodness. "Image-bearer" was the title Adam and Eve were created to wear.

And you and I, sons and daughters, have the honor of bearing the image of God with the seed of goodness planted deep within our hearts.

We are image-bearers. The Creator of all things formed us in our mothers' wombs on purpose with purpose to reflect him on earth. We don't just carry the title of sons and daughters; we have his DNA woven into our bodies and spirits through the breath he breathed into us (Gen. 2:6). I look a lot like my mother. The reflection we have of each other catches people off guard at times. People often think we are sisters, which she loves to hear. I look like my mother, not because I carry the title daughter but because of the DNA that has been passed down to me through her.

On the other hand, I don't look physically like my father, but I still carry his DNA. People know that I am my father's daughter because of how I act, the way I conduct business, my reasoning and thought patterns, and so on. This is an earthly representation of my heavenly relationship.

I not only look like God, but I can act like him too. Through the Holy Spirit, the very being of God is offered to me to live out on earth. God is good, and I have his goodness wired into my DNA. God transferred goodness to me as his daughter. And this trait is cultivated through a life lived yielded to the Holy Spirit. From Abraham, the father of many nations whose seed will be more than the sands on the sea, to David; from David to Jesus; from Jesus to you and me—all one family grafted together with the seed of goodness planted in us to grow and offer to this broken world around us.

The label "image-bearer" isn't a title that is just given and left unmanaged. It is a seed that needs to be cultivated, tended to, and grown. Just as our lives start as a seed, and we grow from the womb to the world, from toddler to teenager, from adult to aging, from life to death, it is a constant process of growth. So it is with our faith. Though we are knit in the womb, formed in the image and goodness of God, we have to choose to live out the purpose God has for us. We must decide to cultivate the seed of him planted deep in our lives. This begins with our salvation, our baptism, and onto the daily spiritual disciplines we participate in, the discipleship we join in, and the way we allow the Holy Spirit to move in our lives.

The growth of our faith, moving from milk to meat, is a process that has to be cared for, watched over, fed, and watered. Remember Harrison's fun little garden? He and I had cared so much for it, watering and nurturing it. But it all came to a halt when we went on vacation. Our family went on a trip in early August when the summer is brutal, and the plants didn't get watered. They dried up, shriveled up, and were no longer able to produce fruit as they should. We have to be ever so attentive to our personal spiritual development: watering and feeding daily the seed that God has planted deep inside us. Because there will be harsh seasons in our lives, and we must prepare to continue in our faith, or it may dry up and become unable to produce fruit.

Had Harrison's plants produced food, then we could have harvested their seeds and created more plants. We have to be continually developing the seeds God has planted in our lives so that we can reach those around us.

Cultivate

If the seed of goodness was planted in our depths, then how do we grow it? How do we continually develop our lives to reflect the image in which we were created? To grow into the goodness the world needs to see, we must cultivate our lives. We live in a very broken world in need of goodness. If we aren't producing goodness, then we can't offer it to those around us. For us to go beyond just doing good things to becoming bearers of goodness, we have to grow in our faith. This type of development takes effort, intentionality, time, and a bit of grit.

If we plant flowers, fruit, vegetables, and trees, we will have to care for each different species individually. Each requires different amounts of water, shade and sun, and assistance. Flowers grow faster and die quicker. Trees grow slowly and can last longer than our lives. As we grow things, we have to spend time, make an effort, and sometimes get a bit dirty to see the fruits of our labor. As we grow in our faith, we must spend time, put forth an effort, and be willing to get a bit dirty to see our fruit grow. But I can assure you, if disciplines are put in place and acted on, the fruit of the spirit will grow, you will bear the goodness of God for others to taste and see.

Several years ago, I was going through a two-year program to receive my master's degree in organizational leadership. One of the classes I took was a spiritual discipline class because every great leader needs spiritual discipline. Let me tell you, this course was excellent and impactful. But it was very theological. Words like "eschatology," "exegesis," and "hermeneutics," among others, were very prevalent. Now you may know what these words mean, but I was a simple public relations major now studying leadership. I didn't understand why we needed such large and foreign words (to me) in the study of spiritual disciplines. I'm still not a fan of those words and prefer their simple definitions—like studying a specific Scripture to understand it or critically thinking about the Scripture. Theological words or not, the idea and implementation of spiritual disciplines is critical to our growth as image-bearers.

Spiritual disciplines are simply things we do to help us grow in the spirit. Disciplines are activities that activate the growth of God's attributes planted inside us. For us to grow into who God created us to be, we must make spiritual disciplines habits in our lives. I spent an entire semester, wrote multiple papers, and commented on many discussion boards regarding this subject, but it is a fundamental and simple act that reaps great rewards. If you do a little research, you can find article after article and numerous books written on this subject, each varying on the number of disciplines in which you can participate. But here's my suggestion: let's not make this complicated; let's simplify the spiritual disciplines so that we have a better chance of following through. There are two simple disciplines that, if intentionally applied to our lives, produce significant growth—and out of those two, many others will naturally develop.

The Word

First, the Word. We must learn to read the Word, study it, and meditate on it daily. If it is for only a few minutes or a few hours, putting the practice into our daily lives makes all the difference in our growth. We all start by reading—merely reading the words printed on the page. Then we must transition to studying those words. I had a wise woman say to me once, "Reading the Word can get boring, but studying it is so much fun." Yes, we start by reading, but we must begin digging deep into its fertile soil. Then we should meditate on it. We think about it. We let it sink into our depths.

One thing every plant needs is water. Without water, there is no survival. As we water plants, the water may at first sit on the soil, but then it will slowly start to sink in, being absorbed by the roots of the plant, bringing growth and life. As we read the Word, it is like water sitting on the soil of our heart; but as we start to study and meditate, the water is absorbed and growth begins to happen. We must consume the Word so we will grow into who God has called us to be for this world. While many Scriptures emphasize the importance of knowing the Word of God, these two spoke strongly to my heart:

All Scripture is breathed out by God and profitable for teaching, for reproof, for correction, and for training in righteousness, that the man of God may be complete, equipped for every good work. (2 Tim. 3:16–17 ESV)

... but his delight is in the law of the Lord
    and on his law he meditates day and night.
He is like a tree
    planted by streams of water
that yields its fruit in season,
    and its leaf does not wither.
In all that he does, he prospers. (Ps. 1:2–3 ESV)

The Word is powerful; it changes us so that we might bring change and life around us. It brings growth, allowing us to bear and offer the fruit of goodness to those we encounter. Whether it is the first thing in the morning, in the car waiting to pick up your kids, in a waiting room, or before bed at night, schedule a time to take in the Word.

Prayer

Second, prayer. Prayer is powerful. We will dive deeper into prayer in another chapter, but prayer is a critical spiritual discipline. Prayer connects us to the one who created us. When we put prayer as a priority, we start to blossom in our purpose. Some prayers are short. Others are long. Some are from a broken state, and others are full of rejoicing. God doesn't care; he just desires for us to take the time to participate.

Another thing plants need is air. Air is critical to their survival. Plants absorb carbon dioxide and release oxygen. This is a cyclical process that if stopped, would kill the plant. As we begin to pray, we open up the line of communication with God. He is faithful to respond, and when he speaks, he breathes life into us. God breathed life into Adam in the garden, and he breathes life into us. When we implement prayer into our daily habit, we continually connect to the breath of life.

The psalmist states, "In the morning, LORD, you hear my voice; in the morning I lay my requests before you and wait in expectantly" (Ps. 5:3 NIV). When we daily lift our voice to the Lord, we can wait in full expectation for him to respond with life. Prayer gives us life; it opens up our hearts to receive the air God is breathing on and into us. Just as a plant both gives and receives air, so we too, having the breath of life breathed into us through prayer, can now give back the goodness we have received.

The Word and prayer are two vital spiritual disciplines needed for our growth as image-bearers. I told you I was going to keep it simple. We can add many other disciplines, such as fasting, worship, fellowship, giving, serving, rest, and disciple-making. But I believe that if you get the Word and prayer down and make them a habit, all the other disciplines will start to come naturally. We need to remember that no matter if we are practicing one or twelve disciplines, they each require intentionality. We must cultivate our spiritual growth. The Holy Spirit has planted deep in us the seeds to bear the fruit, the image of God, but they must be developed. The world around us needs to see the goodness of God, and one way they can do that is through you and me.

Do Good or Bear Good

God didn't make us in his image and expect us to grow into his likeness without sending help. As Jesus walked this earth, he continually taught and demonstrated how to live a life that produces the fruit of the Father. And once he departed, he sent the Holy Spirit to be our comforter and counselor. The Holy Spirit comes alongside us and helps us as we grow into the image of the Father. As we develop the image of God on the inside, it begins to show in our outward appearance and actions. We begin to bear the fruits of the spirit. We move from just doing good to bearing the goodness of God.

Do Good

Everyone can do good. Believer or not, all are capable of doing good for others because God created each of us. There is no good apart from God. So when someone does good, whether she wants to believe it or not, she is acting in the image of her Creator. We see this concept of unexpected people doing good several times in the Bible.

As the Israelites exited Egypt, the Egyptians gave the Hebrew people all the gold and silver they possessed. The Hebrews' God was the one who had caused all the perils they had endured, and the Egyptians weren't "children of God," yet they did something good in the most unlikely of moments. Even the Egyptians were made in the image of God, making their momentary act of goodness a reflection of God's goodness (Exod. 12:35–36).

Then there was King Artaxerxes of Persia. Nehemiah was his cupbearer and served him daily. King Artaxerxes wasn't a believer in the God of Israel, yet he noticed when Nehemiah was sad and questioned him. The king let Nehemiah return to Jerusalem to rebuild the wall. Then he went beyond letting Nehemiah go and also sent letters to ensure Nehemiah's protection. This King of Persia, a nonbeliever yet created in the image of God, still did good, mirroring the goodness of God (Neh. 2).

These two examples express the power of each person made in the image of God. And any good they did solely reflected their Creator and his goodness, whether they knew it or not. But we must move from doing good to bearing good. When we produce goodness, we have something to offer the broken world around us continually. Doing good is momentary—a one-time, singular expression of goodness. But when we produce goodness, through growth as sons and daughters, we become like a tree heavy with fruit, ripe to be picked. Bearing the fruit of goodness allows us to affect more than just one person but instead bring change to our homes, communities, nation, and world.

Bear Good

If we, as believers, struggle to comprehend the goodness of God, then how much more do unbelievers struggle? Yet God placed us in their midst with the power of the Holy Spirit to cultivate the seed of his image planted in us. God desires to use us to display his goodness throughout the earth.

In the book of Genesis, we see the goodness of God displayed through the faithful servant Joseph. Joseph—young and favored, yet despised by his brothers. Their jealousy drove them to throw him into a pit, then sell him as a slave and tell their father he had died. Joseph found himself sold and working for a man named Potiphar as his right-hand man. Potiphar's wife decided she needed Joseph for herself, but Joseph wouldn't concede. Through her lies, Joseph found himself locked up in prison. Even there, he served and found favor. Years later, he would be brought to Pharaoh to interpret a dream. Then he was restored and set as a top leader in Egypt. Famine settled in over the land. Then one day, much to the surprise of Joseph, he was looking at his brothers. His brothers were on their knees in need of food, and Joseph had access to all they needed.

In those many years of hills and valleys, there is one thing we know: Joseph never swayed from developing his life into what God had designed for him. He continually cultivated his image to be one that reflected his God. We know this to be true because Joseph was able to continually offer those around him forgiveness, grace, and mercy, all reflecting the heart of God, his goodness.

Looking at his brothers, Joseph extended goodness, revealing the heart of God. One can only extend goodness if it has been developed and grown over time (Gen. 37–45).

We can also see the goodness of God exhibited in David. David spread the goodness of God to Saul. David, the young shepherd, was called from the field and anointed to be the next king of Israel. David continued his work as a watchman of the sheep, and soon found himself in front of a giant. David slew the giant in front of those whom he would one day reign over. "Saul has slain his thousands, and David his ten thousands!" (1 Sam. 18:7). The woman sang and the people cheered, sending Saul into a fury. Saul, in his rage of jealousy, engaged in the pursuit of David to kill him.

In this chase, David is the one who ended up standing over Saul. David, even with the scene set for him to kill his predecessor and pursuer, stopped. Even when it didn't seem like Saul deserved it, even when it would have been easy to choose death, David extended goodness. David couldn't have offered goodness he hadn't developed. Even while running for his life, David held the words he knew and breathed prayers that fed the seed deep inside. And David began to blossom in the image of God. When he stood face-to-face with his enemy, he offered the goodness of God (1 Sam. 24 and 26).

Both Joseph and David went beyond doing good to bearing good. In the pit and prison and the caves, they allowed the image of God to grow deep inside. They moved from singular moments of goodness to goodness that was on display for all to see. Goodness for all to take from.

Vine of Goodness

Jesus was the epitome of reflecting the image of God to the world around him. Everywhere he went, he bore the fruit of the Spirit, offering the goodness of God for all to see and experience in the land of the living. Everywhere he went, lives changed and healing and freedom were displayed, all because he cultivated his image of God so that he could give it to others. Jesus participated continually in many spiritual disciplines, but you will read that the Word and prayer became his lifelines. Jesus spent as much time as he could in the temple reading from the scrolls and in prayer with his father—and he did this without ceasing. Jesus, in his humanity, cultivated his image of God has he grew and offered it to the world around him. Jesus abided in his father and left us clear instructions: if we want to bear fruit, we must abide in him.

> I am the true vine, and My Father is the gardener. Every branch in Me that does not bear fruit, He takes away; and every branch that bears fruit, He trims so that it may bear more fruit. You are already clean because of the word I have spoken to you. Abide in Me, and I will abide in you. The branch cannot itself produce fruit, unless it abides on the vine. Likewise, you cannot produce fruit unless you abide in Me.
>
> I am the vine; you are the branches. The one who abides in Me, and I in him, bears much fruit; for apart from Me, you can do nothing. If anyone does not abide in Me, he is thrown away like a branch and is dried up. Such branches are picked up and thrown into the fire and burned.
>
> If you abide in Me and My words abide in you, ask whatever you wish, and it shall be done for you. In this My Father is glorified, that you bear much fruit and so prove to be My disciples. (John 15:1–8)

It's the will of Jesus that we be forever connected to him, growing in him so that we can bear the fruit of the Spirit, drawing the lost and broken into the vine. We can never expect to offer something we do not have. There are people all around us hurting, sick, and in pain, questioning the goodness of God. And God has called us to reflect and extended him to this world. But we cannot offer the fruit of goodness if we aren't bearing it, and we cannot offer Absolute Goodness if we aren't connected to it.

As God knit us in the womb of our mother, the goodness of God was planted deep inside each of us. And as we grow in this world, we must move from just doing good to bearing good. We do this by ensuring our lives are connected to the vine of Absolute Goodness. Then we must allow the Holy Spirit to flow through us as we cultivate our seed through the Word and prayer, causing the fruit of the Spirit to be on display for all to see. Everywhere Jesus went, people were drawn to him because he offered something different to them, something their souls were craving. Everywhere we go—church, the doctor, the store, the sports field, everywhere—souls are craving what we have.

So let us ever so faithfully cultivate the image of God—his goodness, planted deep inside us—so that through the power of the Holy Spirit, we can bear the goodness of God for the world to see, leading them to Absolute Goodness.

Chapter Eight Reflection

1. As an image-bearer of God, take a moment to reflect on his characteristics and evaluate yourself and the way you bear his image.

2. Read Galatians 5:22–23.

3. Do you occasionally live the fruit of the Spirit, or do you consistently bear the fruit of the Spirit?

4. Do you have a set time every day that you take to read and mediated on the Word and pray? If not, I encourage you to evaluate your day and plan a time where you can cultivate who God has created you to be.

nine

My Goodness Is Working

We can see hope in the midst of hopelessness. We can see peace in the midst of chaos. We have a hope that the world does not have. We can see clearly that all things work together for the good of them that love Him and are called according to His purpose.

—Priscilla Shirer

THE GOODNESS OF GOD MOVES LIKE A CURRENT—continually running in every season and every moment of our lives. This very moment, God is good and is doing good (Ps. 119:68), and he is working all things together for good on behalf of those who love him (Rom. 8:28). But that doesn't mean we must wait to see goodness. Often, we loosely quote Scripture, saying, "God will turn this for good." We say this to ourselves and to others in an attempt to remain positive in painful moments. When we quote the Scripture this way, though, we see goodness as some futuristic event we will have to wait to experience. Our mindset points to the idea that God will send his goodness later to fix the terrible situation we are presently facing. But what if we changed our mindset? What if we saw the goodness of God in this very moment through the comfort and power of the Holy Spirit? Knowing goodness goes before us offers peace. Knowing goodness follows us ushers in grace. Knowing we have experienced goodness in our past brings freedom. But we can't forget the here and now. God is a present God; his goodness is working at this moment doing good for you and me, and we have the opportunity to bask in it.

As the children of God exited their bondage in Egypt and set out on their journey to the promise, God wanted to reveal some things to his children. There in the dry season, the wilderness season, God spoke clearly to his people. God gave the Hebrews a pretty big task: construct the tent of meeting. This building project came with clear and detailed instructions. One of the items on the list to make was the Ark of the Covenant. This Ark represented the presence of God. The priest would carry the Ark as the Israelites traveled on their journey. If ever a doubt of goodness arose, they just needed to look up toward the Ark and remember God was moving with them. His goodness traveled with them, worked among them, and did good in them and for them (Exod. 25–31).

Then God sent our Absolute Goodness, Jesus, to move through the earth, revealing the goodness of God. Jesus regularly moved from place to place, person to person, ushering in the presence of God, uncovering the goodness of God. Jesus made it known that the goodness of God is always doing good and working good on our behalf.

As Jesus departed, God, in his continual goodness, sent the Holy Spirit. The Holy Spirit moves with us, speaks to us, guides us, comforts us, protects us, reveals to us, and so much more. Every moment of every day, the sweet goodness of the Holy Spirit is doing good because God is good.

We have access to see the present goodness moving in our lives; we just need to take a moment to view it. We get busy with life and become distracted and miss goodness. We get caught up in whatever emotional moment we are engaged in and forget there is goodness present. From the mountaintop moments to the lonely valleys, goodness is ever before our eyes if we allow the Holy Spirit to reveal it.

God is so good to give us the grace to see and experience goodness in our past. But I can assure you that he doesn't want you to miss the goodness of God at this very moment. It's so easy to do. I am guilty of it. But how much more peaceful would our lives be if we allowed the Holy Spirit to continually reveal the purposeful, working, present goodness of God in our lives?

- God is good in the vows of "death do us part" and in the decree of divorce.
- God is good in the union of conception, through joys and struggles of a growing womb, and in the delivery of a promise.
- God is good in the sound of a muffled heartbeat, and he is good when all that echoes is silence.
- God is good in sweet success and amid the fog of failure.
- God is good in the pleasantries of promotion and the lag of layoff.
- God is good when we breathe a sigh of relief and when the breath has been knocked from us.
- God is good in the joy of life and in the grips of grief.

There is not one moment when God stops being good. There is not a single moment when the goodness of God is not flooding our lives, but life has a way of causing us to miss goodness. But our good Father offers us access to the Holy Spirit, who in the highest of highs and lowest of lows can nudge our hearts, open our eyes, and uncover the goodness of God flooding our lives like a stream of water. There are countless examples of the goodness of God working in the present moment throughout the Bible, so I want to take a little time to venture through a few of them.

Daniel and the Three Friends

King Nebuchadnezzar of Babylon ruled over Jerusalem and Judah. Daniel, Shadrach, Meshach, and Abednego were taken as chosen sons of Israel to serve in the king's palace. They were capable men, described as handsome and full of wisdom and knowledge. They were men who loved their God. During this time, King Nebuchadnezzar started to dream dreams that left him unsettled and confused. He sought magicians, sorcerers, and enchanters—almost anyone he could find to interpret the dreams. None could do the job. King Nebuchadnezzar grew angry until Daniel stepped in. God revealed to him the dream and the meaning, and then Daniel explained the revelation to the king. The king was pleased and appointed Daniel to rule and serve from the king's palace, and his three buddies were elected to the affairs over Babylon (Dan. 1 and 2).

The Three Friends

Then King Nebuchadnezzar came up with what seemed to be a good idea to him and built a golden statue for all to worship. I imagine this put Shadrach, Meshach, and Abednego in a tense situation. The king had declared clear instructions regarding the worship of his new trophy. The ordinance stated that every time they heard the sound of music, all must fall and worship the golden image. If anyone failed to obey, he would find himself cast into a burning fiery furnace. Shadrach, Meshach, and Abednego wouldn't submit to the idea of idol worship, and their actions were made known to the king. He became furious and had them brought to him. Then King Nebuchadnezzar grew enraged when, even in front of him, the three friends still wouldn't bow down to his image. That is when the king told his servants to heat the furnace seven times hotter than usual and ordered some of his men to cast the men into the fire.

The three friends had experienced the goodness of God going before them; they knew God to be absolutely good, but they needed to experience the God who does good right now. They needed goodness to be worked out right then, not just hope for goodness to work good eventually. As they were tossed into the furnace, goodness showed up. Right in the middle of the fire, in what could have been a moment of anger, grief, confusion, pain, and death, the current of goodness flowed through their lives, making itself known (Dan. 3).

Daniel

And we can't forget about Daniel. Daniel grew into a distinguished official, high above the other officials, and was set to become the most senior official. Other officials weren't pleased with the favor bestowed on Daniel, so they looked for a complaint against him; and when they couldn't find one, they conspired to create one. The jealous officials convinced the king (now King Darius) to sign an agreement, which stated that no one could make a petition to any god or man except the king for thirty days.

Daniel knew the ordinance the king had enacted, but he continued to pray as he had always done. Those looking to find fault saw him continue to pray faithfully and took the matter to the king. The king felt distraught because his now-favored official must be thrown into the den of lions. Daniel was cast into the lion's den, and then the opening was covered with a stone. Daniel, like his friends, needed his God who does good to do good right then. He needed to see the current of goodness move right in that very moment. Goodness showed up and shut the mouths of the lions for Daniel (Dan. 6).

The Disciples

The disciples received the Holy Spirit in Acts 2. From that moment, they went out and proclaimed the message of Jesus until their time on earth was over. But during their journeys, they experienced the highs and lows of this life. They endured warm welcomes by some and passionate persecution by others. But, through it all, they allowed the Holy Spirit to guide them, speak to them, and reveal the goodness of God working every moment of their lives.

Peter and John went from the mountaintop of a mass conversion and the healing of a lame beggar to the valley of jail in a short amount of time. But even then, the goodness of God was working and moving. God was doing good. Peter and John didn't get distracted by what might happen or what was happening. They didn't let fear, anger, or bitterness set in. They kept their eyes on their Absolute Goodness and allowed the Holy Spirit to empower them, revealing the present goodness of God (Acts 2–4).

Then there is Stephen. Stephen overflowed with the Holy Spirit, allowing him to fulfill his calling. Yet some men decided to lie about what Stephen had been preaching. So he was taken to the Sanhedrin, where false witnesses spoke out against him. Even amid these powerful people, Stephen rejected the fear of death, the anger of lies, and the frustration of injustice, and embraced the goodness of God working on his behalf. Stephen allowed the Holy Spirit to use him to speak the goodness of God to those he stood in front of. The people who listened became enraged, but Stephen, through the Holy Spirit, gazed up, and saw the glory of God and his Absolute Goodness, Jesus, standing at the right hand of the Father. In the middle of his pain, the goodness of God worked on his behalf. Even in the middle of martyrdom, the goodness of God was still present (Acts 6–7).

Later, Peter, once again, was arrested. Peter was bound with two chains between two soldiers when goodness showed up. An angel of the Lord appeared and told Peter to get up, get dressed, and follow him. After they left the prison and began walking on a narrow street, the angel left him. Then Peter said, "Now I know for real that the Lord has sent His angel and delivered me from the hand of Herod and from the all that the Judean people were expecting" (Acts 12:11). There in the middle of prison, while Peter was chained to two guards, goodness showed up. The goodness of God presently moved in Peter's life. He didn't have to wait to experience goodness. It was actively working in the present moment.

Paul

The goodness of God guided Paul, went before him, and followed him continually. But Paul also experienced this present goodness, steadily moving in his journey to spread the good news. If we revisit the story of Paul and the shipwreck, which we read in Chapter Five, we will see that there is more goodness to experience. The goodness of God guided Paul through the storm that left them shipwrecked on the island of Malta. At Malta, the men from the ship embraced the shore wet, exhausted, and I'm sure a little overwhelmed by all that had just happened. The people of the island welcomed them. They built a warm fire because it was raining and cold. And as Paul placed the gathered brushwood on the fire, a viper latched on to his hand.

The islanders saw the snake hanging from his hand and, believing it was a sign, thought he was a murderer. But Paul shook the snake off his hand into the fire and experienced no side effects from the snakebite. Talk about God doing good. Right there at that moment, Paul needed the goodness of God to be on display.

Paul didn't just need goodness to be present for his own sake and health; he needed it to be present for the people.

Paul was then led to the house of a nearby official, where he laid his hands on the official's father to be healed. The goodness of God was active, working all things together not just for Paul but for the islanders as well. The goodness of God was present and working for all to see (Acts 28).

Goodness Every Moment

These are just a few stories that reflect the goodness of God actively working in the present moments of his children. In those dire, immediate moments, God is still good, and his goodness is available right then. As our hearts turn in love toward the Father, he is actively working things together for our good. There are some situations where it is easy to see goodness and others where it feels like we may be only staring at a speck of light in a dark room. But this goodness, I can assure you, is working. It is present in every moment of our lives—the dire, as we just read, the successful, the mundane, and the failing.

Mundane

A couple of weeks ago, my older boys were at school, and Harrison was home with me for the day. I need to get him settled so I could sit in my office and write. I turned on his favorite show, pulled out his favorite toys, and made sure a snack and water sat close by. But as soon as I sat down, I heard, "Mommy, you can come sit and play with me?" My response should've been joy and excitement for the opportunity to sit and play. But the thoughts in my head were on the deadline for this book. Unengaged, I sat on the floor with him and attempted to play.

Sitting there half-heartedly playing, a little frustrated, the Holy Spirit spoke to me. The Spirit nudged me to remember a time when I didn't get to sit with my boys on the floor and play because I worked outside the home. Then I remembered a time when I didn't sit with my boys to play because I suffered from such severe postpartum depression that I didn't do anything but survive. I was reminded of past moments so that I could see the goodness of God working in the present moment. The goodness of God sometimes comes in the moments when we spend our time playing with our messy kids on the floor. The goodness of God comes in the moment of cooking a meal for the family to enjoy together. These little, mundane moments we take for granted are moments when goodness is ever-present and working.

Every part of the Bible contains layer upon layer of guidance and teaching—and that includes the mundane moments too. After a long day, the disciples were hungry. The thousands of people sitting on the hillside were surely hungry too. But there was nothing to feed the five thousand men and those with them. They found a couple of fish and five loaves of bread that a boy had brought with him. Jesus blessed the minimal, and it fed the multitude. What sweet goodness in the miracle! But what comes next is so important. After the miracle, after everyone was fed, the time came for cleanup.

The disciples, now with full stomachs, and everyone who was coming down from the awe of the multiplication miracle find it is time to clean up. Each disciple grabbed a basket, walked around the multitude of people, and picked up the fragments of food left behind, filling twelve baskets. It's easy to see goodness in the miracle moments; but in the mundane, we have to be intentional about seeing it. The disciples moved from group to group, area to area, cleaning up after five thousand plus people, picking up bread, fish, bread, fish, bread, fish, and on and on. But in the tedious moment came the provision of twelve full baskets of food (Matt. 14:13–21).

We must not get weary in the day-in and day-out movements of our lives. When washing dishes, sweeping the floor, making the bed, folding the laundry, and cleaning up, don't miss goodness. In the early morning commute, lunch at the office, and the tired drive home, don't miss goodness. In the repetitive movements of life, don't miss goodness. It is present. It is active. It is working. Just pause a moment to see it, to revel in it.

Failure

No one likes the word "failure." We spend our lives doing everything we can to stay as far away as possible from that seemingly dirty word. Yet in all our efforts, we still find ourselves having failed at one time or another.

- We fail tests.
- We fail in business.
- We fail at parenting.
- We fail at marriage.
- We fail all the time.

I have realized that when we fail, we tend to embrace shame, self-pity, fear, or anxiety before we look for goodness.

I am so guilty of this. There was a period of time, after having our sweet second boy, Collin, when I suffered from postpartum depression coupled with post-traumatic stress disorder. It was a rough combination that left me failing as a mother and a wife. I failed at almost everything. And instead of running toward goodness, I embraced the fear that relentlessly lingered. I was left unfulfilled and feeling hopeless. I missed goodness in the middle of failing, but I didn't have too. Yes, God worked all things together for good—thank you, Jesus—but in those very moments, there was goodness available for me to cling to that I overlooked.

And just the other day, I had a small but total mom fail. All in one day, I forgot to take Collin to a critical doctor's appointment, showed up late to pick the boys up from school, and forgot to attend a parent-teacher conference. Now, none of those things are the worst thing, but doing them all in one day made it feel like a totally unsuccessful day. As the day closes, when we are tired, shortcomings are highlighted in our minds, and, unfortunately, we dwell there. We start to embrace shame for messing up, the anxiety of what people might think, and guilt for our mistakes. But all the while, even in our messy failures, goodness is available for us to experience.

That day, unlike years past, I rejected shame and embraced the goodness of grace. The goodness of God was with me, working for me even in my mishaps—I just needed to see it. I saw my good Father offering a stream of goodness in the form of grace, and I jumped in. Later that evening, I shared with the boys my faults for the day, and, once again, the goodness of grace was extended. My sweet boys told me, "It's okay, Mom. You have so much going on; it happens," and they offered me sweet boy hugs and then told me I could go to bed early if I needed. Significant failures, small mishaps—our good Father is still doing good. Goodness is available. We just have to see it and embrace it.

I can't help but think of the prophet Elijah when I think of goodness in the middle of our failures. Elijah was a mighty man of God. He seemed fearless and full of faith. There came a time when the tension between the prophet of God and the prophets of Baal rose, which led to a showdown on Mount Carmel. There atop the mount, 450 prophets of Baal faced off against one prophet of God, Elijah. There, they would settle once and for all who was the One true living God. The prophets of Baal prepared their bull and began to call out to their God to send down fire. And nothing happened. All the while, Elijah taunted them. Now it was Elijah's turn. He fixed the altar. He placed the wood, the bull, and then poured water on top. Then he prayed, and fire fell and consumed the offering, wood, stones, dust, and water. It was settled. With that faith, it doesn't seem like Elijah was failing.

But it wasn't too long after this that Jezebel heard of this, heard of Elijah killing Baal's prophets, so she sent a threatening word to Elijah. And just like that, the man who called down fire from heaven in faith was fleeing in fear for his life. Elijah fled to the wilderness and wanted to die. While there, an angel provided food and drink for him. He then traveled to the mountain of God in Horeb and hid in a cave. And there, the Lord began to speak to Elijah. A mighty wind blew, the earth shook, a fire burned, but God's voice wasn't in those. After that, there was a whisper—the voice of God.

Elijah experienced great success as a servant of the Lord, but he also felt the failure. The fear of man gripped him and left him running from his purpose. But even in this breakdown, the goodness of God was present, active, and working. The goodness of God sent an angel to provide for Elijah in his despair. The goodness of God came in a soft, gentle whisper to touch his aching heart and mind. But Elijah had to choose to embrace the goodness that was before him. He had to choose to eat and drink of the provision. He had to choose to listen carefully to the voice that was softly speaking to him. The goodness of God was ever-present in Elijah's valley, working and moving (1 Kings 18–19).

Success

Everyone's standard for success is different; but even among the differences, success is something we all desire to experience. Success is something that our world strives for and longs to live in. Over the years, my definition and idea of success have evolved. Now I believe success is living out your God-given purpose. If you spent a little time with me, you would hear me say, "You were created on purpose for a purpose to impact the kingdom." I believe with everything in me that you find success when you are fulfilling your purpose.

But even in the highlights of success, feeling like you are on top of the world, we can miss the goodness of God. It seems a bit strange to think we might miss goodness in the best moments of life. Sometimes pride creeps in, or maybe it is just complacency—but it can happen.

This happened with King Saul. God called Samuel to anoint Saul as the ruler over his children. Saul, full of purpose, found success in living out this purpose. But over time, at the height of his life, Saul missed the goodness of God. Saul started to live by what felt good and right for him. He became prideful and complacent in his purpose and missed the voice of God. Saul missed the goodness of God at work in every moment of his life, guiding and directing him as he led the nation.

In contrast, there is David. He humbly and patiently waited to take his rightful place as the king of Israel. He, like Saul, was fulfilling his God-given purpose. David experienced failures during his tenure, but he lived a successful life because he faithfully fulfilled his purpose. God called David a man after his own heart (1 Sam. 13:14; Acts 13:22). David's life is a stark contrast to Saul's. We must learn to see the goodness of God working and moving in the right-now moments of our lives. When we have a heart that longs to chase after God, in the highest of highs or the lowest of lows, we will have eyes to see the goodness of God working on our behalf.

David declared in Psalms, "You are good and keep doing good—teach me Your decrees" (Ps. 119:68). Our God is oh so good, and his goodness is endless. It is moving like a stream through our lives. He is continually doing good for those who love him and are called according to his purpose. We can never completely comprehend how much good God does every day, but let's be aware of the moments we find ourselves in—the dire, the mundane, the failing, and the successful moments. And in each of these moments, may our hearts be reaching after the heart of God, taking time to step into the stream of goodness flowing through every moment of our lives.

Chapter Nine Reflection

1. Is your mindset one that just believes God will work things for good, or is it one that is seeking to see goodness in this very moment?

2. Seeing goodness work in this very moment often requires us to pause. Take this moment to pause and ask the Holy Spirit to reveal his goodness in this very day and moment. Ask the Holy Spirit to help your heart and mind to be sensitive to his nudging and revelation of goodness in the present moments.

ten

My Goodness Is a Conversation

Prayer is not monologue, but dialogue; God's voice is its most essential part. Listening to God's voice is the secret of the assurance that He will listen to mine.

—Andrew Murray

I LOVE TO TALK! I LOVE TO TALK ALL THE TIME AND to anyone. While growing up, it was a common occurrence for me to receive some sort of disciplinary action because I talked too much at school. Even now, as I sit in a church service, seminar, or meeting, I still find myself wanting to whisper something to the person sitting next to me, even if I don't know them. I don't care if you are a stranger or if I've known you my entire life; I would love to talk to you. I received my degree in public relations, and one of the most helpful lessons I learned in that career was to read all types of magazines and books. One company I worked for subscribed to magazines ranging from *Cosmopolitan* to *Popular Mechanics* and anything in between. We would read articles in various fields of work, learning even the smallest news or interesting detail. Why? Because we never knew whom we would be sitting next to on an airplane, at an appointment, or in a meeting, nor what their background might be. And if I wanted to carry on a conversation with them, I needed to have something in my pocket to talk to them about. This is a tactic I frequently practice. I am always looking for things to keep in my pocket so that no matter whom I am sitting next to, I can engage in a friendly conversation.

The idea of conversation is different for everyone. Some of us are more extroverted, while others are more introverted. But no matter where you fall on the social scale, not only are conversations a social requirement; we desire communication with others. While I tend to have a lot of discussions, and others may like to say only a few words, conversations are necessary. But more importantly, we must know that conversations are a gift.

God ultimately displayed his goodness in the most significant gift he gave to us: relationship. He gave us his goodness, Jesus, to mend our broken relationship so we could continue living in his goodness through a right relationship with him. Any therapist will tell you the biggest problem in relationships is communication. God gave the good gift of relationship, but if we want the connection to stay healthy, we must learn to communicate. Our relationship with God doesn't go south because of him, but because we doubt him due to lies we have believed. "Whenever he speaks lies he is just being himself—for he is a liar and the father of lies" (John 8:44). We believe lies the enemy is continually firing our way, and then we doubt God and his goodness. We long to see the goodness of God in the land of the living, but if we want to experience it, we must engage in conversation.

We must take advantage of the goodness he has given us, offering us the engagement of a never-ending conversation with our friend. Scripture says to "pray without ceasing" (1 Thess. 5:17 NKJV). But that doesn't mean we have to spend hours on end locked in our closet praying. Yes, you do need to find yourself behind closed doors on your face before the Lord. But God gave us all good gifts. A few of my blessings are my husband, three boys, a purpose, a church, and so many more. I must steward those gifts, which means I cannot stay in my closet all day—though those gifts are often what drive me to my closet. (Ha!) I get to drive my boys to their activities, work at the church, clean my house, and fulfill my purpose. So, praying without ceasing is more than a closet prayer. It's living with a prayer on my heart and a conversation rolling in my mind with the Holy Spirit at all times. I'm not anywhere close to the *without ceasing* level, but I am doing my best to continue the conversation.

When I keep this chat between Jesus and me going, I am continually walking in and experiencing the goodness of God. This continual exchange keeps my shield of faith up and my armor secure so that I can stand and ward off the fiery darts that are guaranteed to shoot my way. The enemy is relentless, but God gave us a way to experience his goodness that never ceases. When we pray without ceasing, when we continue the conversation, we experience his never-ending goodness. We must enter into the goodness of conversation with our Creator, opening our eyes to see God's goodness flowing through and holding our world together.

Counterfeit Conversations

Too often, we have counterfeit conversations and made up dialogues that leave us empty and unfulfilled. We create conversations with other people in our minds of what we should say, or what we might say, or what we could have said. All based on what we believe should be said or what we want the other party to reply. We are the actor in all the parts of the conversation. We replay the mind chat over and over, with each version varying just a bit in preparation for an anticipated discussion that will probably never really happen. Or we do this as a way to rewrite in our minds a conversation that has already passed.

Growing up, my dad always made my brother and I listen to Zig Ziglar on cassette tapes. We would roll our eyes every time he pushed a cassette into the tape deck of our car. But on one of these occasions, I remember hearing Zig say something about talking to oneself. He was encouraging listeners to talk to themselves, because it made them more intelligent. I was around eight or nine when I heard this, so I don't remember all the details of the talk, but I remember thinking, *I'm going to talk to myself, because I want to be smart.* And I did. I talked to myself often. My young imagination ran wild with many stories, which turned into my learning to encourage myself.

Zig Ziglar was not talking about counterfeit conversations. He was talking about encouraging yourself, not creating false worlds in the hope that they may come true or may change the past. But the best way to encourage yourself isn't talking just to yourself but also talking to Jesus. But we speak to ourselves in made-up conversations that don't include Jesus, and that leaves us unfulfilled and never encouraged.

We start telling a story, replaying a scenario, or processing a situation in our mind; but too often, we do one of two things. One, we play things out in our thoughts and pretend like we can solve the situation on our own, never inviting God into the conversation. We engage in chat with ourselves like God can't hear it. Or, two, we ask God into the discussion on a limited basis. We have a one-sided conversation; we talk and talk but never allow God to speak back to us. And when we feel like God might speak up, we shut the conversation off.

We must move away from fake conversations. We need to leave the made-up stories and scenarios at the foot of the cross. Scripture says to "demolish every deceptive fantasy that opposes

God" (2 Cor. 10:5 TPT). We must be willing to cast down the counterfeit conversations and engage in a discussion of goodness with our good Father. God desires to speak into every part of our lives, but we have to let him talk—and we must be willing to listen.

The Bible itself is one giant, recorded conversation. It's living and breathing, and every time we read it, we are entering into conversation. Inside the Bible are numerous conversations from which we can glean. There is no better place to start than with one of the first recorded conversations.

Garden Conversation

God is so good that he created a conversation with us, knowing we would fail, and yet he still wants to talk to us. The enemy wants us to believe that if we mess up, if we don't pray right, if we don't pray enough, then we shouldn't pray at all because we have disappointed God. Friend, let me tell you, that's trash right there! And what do we do with trash? We throw it away! God knew we would fail big time. God knew we would struggle. In his goodness, he still desires to talk to us. He always wants a conversation with us. It's in those conversations that God can reveal the depths of his goodness in our past, present, and future. We see this happen in one of the first conversations of the Bible.

We read of the serpent twisting the words of God and attempting to distort the goodness of God. Unfortunately, Eve and Adam fell for the lie. And what do we see happen after that? Shame. Though they had always been naked, they suddenly became wrapped in shame, and Adam and Eve ran and hid. They seemed scared to continue in the relationship they once had with the Father. They didn't want to see him face-to-face anymore; they weren't sure what to say to him. They no longer felt worthy of being in conversation with their Creator.

But God still wanted to be in communication with his children, because he is that good. Now, the conversation that followed wasn't an easy one, but it was a necessary one. God had a conversation that was infused with discipline and love—a conversation that expressed and would forever echo his love and goodness. He covered their bodies with sacrifice and removed them from the garden, and they entered the wilderness of the world. But even then, God continued his conversation with his children. The garden conversation was meant to be forever face-to-face, but sin has now shunned us to the wilderness. Yet God still meets us there in our wilderness to have the conversation of his goodness (Gen. 3).

Wilderness Conversation

Another short conversation that reflects many conversations people have with God is one between Hagar and God. Hagar found herself a broken woman, rejected by the ones who broke her. Because of Sarai's lack of trust in God, she used Hagar to conceive a baby. Once Hagar became pregnant, Sarai loathed and rejected Hagar. Hagar did what she was forced to do—she ran. She ran away from her painful and challenging circumstances, just as so many of us do—whether it is physically, mentally, or emotionally. We run just like Hagar. We try to run away, and we find ourselves in the wilderness alone and broken.

When she ran, I am sure she wanted to blame Abram and Sarai and probably wanted to question whether God was still good. Hagar was a woman, and her thoughts were no different than yours and mine. I imagine she was replaying many times over in her head conversations she had with Sarai and Abram. I imagine she was creating false narratives in the hopes of making herself feel better. I can also guarantee you that when she ran to the wilderness, the enemy was waiting to pounce on her broken heart. That is where the enemy loves to make his move: in our dry isolation. He made his first move in the garden, which sent Adam and Eve to the wilderness. Even now, the enemy has set up camp in our wilderness, waiting for us to be shaken and run from our place of peace to the wilderness.

But we read that an angel of the Lord found Hagar and asked her a question. The decision to respond laid in Hagar's court. We must know that God is always willing to engage in conversation with us. He is faithful to draw us near to him continually; he is that good. He will meet us in the wilderness, even when we are running, and start a conversation. But, we have the choice to respond. Hagar had the option to reply. Hagar chose to engage in the conversation. She didn't have too, but she did. She probably didn't feel like it, but she pushed beyond what she was feeling, beyond the lies the enemy fired her way, and responded. It was up to Hagar to reject the fake conversation in her head and embrace conversation with the Creator.

We must embrace and engage in conversation with God. It might have felt more comfortable for Hagar to not talk to God, but God wanted to reveal himself to her. Had Hagar rejected the conversation God wanted to have with her, she would have missed the revelation of goodness. God wanted to do something incredible in Hagar's life. She would have missed the eye-opening experience of knowing God is the God who sees. In the wilderness, in the middle of her brokenness, in her attempt to run, God started a conversation. Hagar engaged, and her eyes awoke to God's goodness. "So she called to ADONAI who was speaking to her, 'You are the God who sees me.' For she said, 'Would I have gone here indeed looking for Him who looks after me?'" (Gen. 16:13).

That wilderness conversation opened new hope for Hagar. That nugget of goodness is what would sustain her for the times that were coming. That conversation was a conversation of goodness.

If we want to know God and his goodness, we must engage in conversation. In the middle of our broken lives, stranded desperately in the wilderness, we must join the conversation. God's goodness is illuminated when we communicate with him.

Redemptive Conversation

The enemy came into the garden and started a new conversation that forever keeps us running to the wilderness in shame, hiding from God, feeling as if we may not be worthy of a conversation with our Father. As we read above, we see this same scenario played out with Hagar. Hagar was driven to the wilderness in desperation, but instead of allowing shame to overshadow, she allowed God to speak to her situation. Time and time again, we will find ourselves in a situation that causes us to feel disappointment, shock, shame, hurt, anxiety, and fear, to name a few. These circumstances will make us want to run to the wilderness and will try to keep up from engaging with our good God. We know that Jesus, our Absolute Goodness, came to redeem all that the enemy has tried to steal from us.

Jesus shows us how to defeat the enemy while engaging in conversation with the Father. Matthew details Jesus's wilderness experience. We must understand that nothing forced Jesus into the wilderness; he willingly went on our behalf. There in the wilderness, where the enemy loves to prey, Satan came to Jesus and began his conversation. We must notice that the enemy engaged the same way here as he did with Adam and Eve. It's a twisting of the words that is a partial truth spun into a lie. Satan posed three twisted statements, and Jesus replied three times with Scripture.

We know that Hagar had a conversation with God. And I am telling you to have a conversation with God. But it appears as if Jesus did the opposite. Here's the deal: Jesus knew you would find yourself in the wilderness, having a conversation with the enemy, and so he came to teach us how to overcome those conversations. The only way we can do that is if we are actively engaged in a conversation with our Father. Jesus tells us he does not say anything unless the Father instructs it, which means he is in a conversation that never ceases with his Father (John 5:19, 8:28, 12:49). So when Jesus was in the wilderness, we don't read of the dialogue Jesus had with God, but we know it happened because of what Jesus has said (Matt. 4:1–11).

Through this communication, we see God is a good God who empowers us to be overcomers. Hagar entered into conversation with God. Jesus conversed with his Father without ceasing. We, too, must engage in conversation with God in the garden and the wilderness, knowing that God will reveal himself to us, sharing his great goodness.

There are conversations of joy and pain, discipline and pardon, anger and praise, desperation and rejoicing. The conversations are endless, and there is no discussion that God is scared to have. God wants you to participate in the goodness of communication. When we do, we open our hearts and minds to experience his goodness in every part of our lives.

Conversation with God is so good that it creates this beautiful, contrasting picture. Our prayers rise to heaven like incense burning. They are a pleasing aroma to God that move his heart. They continually flow upward like a beautiful pillar of smoke rising from a chimney on a cold winter's night. But just as beautiful and peaceful as our conversations are, they are also fierce. Our prayers are the sound of war wreaking havoc in hell. It is the call of us going to war and walking in the power God has given us. The goodness of conversation with God goes beyond our imagination. Our words never end. They continue forever and ever. The words of God who created this world and sealed it with goodness never cease. His words endure forever, holding this life together.

Our words continue through the atmosphere forever. Our words continually rise and war.

Deciphering the Voices

When we enter into a conversation with God, we must learn how to decipher the different voices we hear. When we stop to listen to what God has to say, he is faithful to speak, but we must know how to weed out not only the voice of the enemy but our voice too. The enemy will be there speaking, trying to create interference in your communication with the Almighty. He will utter phrases that look like truth but are, in fact, lies. And if the enemy can't get you that way, he will try to convince you that what you heard was something you made up, and it wasn't God speaking. How do we decipher God's voice from our own and the enemy's? There are a couple of ways to be sure of what you are hearing.

The voice of God will never contradict his Word. What God speaks to your spirit will always line up with the written Word of God. If what you are hearing goes against the Bible, that is a half-truth from the enemy. There was a time in our marriage when we hit a bit of a rough patch. Brad had done something that had hurt me. With my heart hurting and my marriage a bit shaken, I took the matter to Jesus. While I was in this conversation with Jesus, I heard the phrase, *You don't deserve this; you deserve so much more.*

Because I was in conversation with God, it would have been easy to believe what I heard was God. But even when we pray, the enemy is fighting to win the battle of the conversation. That phrase came from the pit of hell; it was trash, and I threw it away. In reality, there was a bit of truth to what the enemy said—I didn't deserve what had happened—but the enemy was attempting to use a half-truth to captivate my mind and turn it away from God's truth. The real truth is that God created Brad and me for each other, and even though I was hurting, we are in this marriage for good, to do good, and to bring glory to God. We must know the truth, the real absolute truth, or we will have a hard time deciphering God's voice from the lies masquerading as truth.

God's voice brings love, peace, acceptance, and correction. You can guarantee you have engaged in a fake conversation with the enemy if you feel fear, anxiety, shame, or condemnation. What often happens in our conversations with God is that we will take the issue at hand to him and ask for his peace, guidance, love, grace, and mercy. Then, when we leave the conversation with God, we will engage in a fake conversation, and anxiety will set it, and fear will overtake us. And we never even realize we started participating in a different discussion. We must take note of what we are feeling so we can decipher the truth of what voice we are hearing and what conversation we are engaged in.

We must become intimately acquainted with the voice of God, so we can still have a conversation with him amid the noise and chaos around us. When we engage in conversation and hear him amongst the lies the enemy is throwing our way, we see the goodness of God revealed like never before. It's in the chaos of life that the enemy wants you to doubt God's goodness; but in that very moment, if we will press in and engage in a two-way conversation, God's goodness will be exposed.

Engage in the Conversation

One of my favorite conversations is recorded in 2 Samuel 5. David asks God a couple of questions: "Should I go up against the Philistines? Will You give them over into my hand?" (v. 19). David engages in a small conversation with the Lord. David needed to know what his next step should be. He desired to do what the Lord wanted him to do, so he simply asked and then listened. God will always respond to us; he is continually communicating with us. But we must become not just talkers but listeners, too.

God replies to David, "Go up, for I will certainly give the Philistines over into your hand" (v. 19). Because David tuned his ear to what God was saying, he heard clear instruction and then obeyed. When we hear the Spirit of the Lord speak to us, we must learn to obey. God didn't give David a step-by-step instruction, but he did give David his word.

When David enters into conversation with God, it is a multi-step process. David opens up to God and asks a question. We must open our mouths, pour out our hearts, present our requests, and ask our questions. But there comes a time, as it did with David, when we must stop talking and listen. David allowed God to speak back to him, and we too must allow the Spirit of the Lord to respond to our hearts and trust what we hear. And then we must be willing to obey, to do the thing God has asked us to do. There was so much goodness in the simple conversation David had with God, but it would have been missed if David hadn't engaged, listened, and obeyed. Day by day, we must engage in the conversation with God and let the next bit of goodness unfold before our eyes. We will never experience the fullness of how good God truly is if we don't participate in a conversation with him. We must be willing to engage, ready to listen, and eager to obey.

Conversations with ourselves are easy. Conversations with God, where we are the only ones talking, are relaxed. But those easy conversations miss the beautiful dichotomy of God's simply complex nature. We must move from discussions that list everything out for God to conversations where we listen and obey. We must train ourselves to know God's voice, reject the enemy's false narrative, and embrace the simply complex conversations with God. It's there in the wilderness conversation where we received the revelation of God's goodness.

I want to leave you with this: the goodness of God is more profound than we could ever comprehend and does more than we could ever imagine. If we're going to experience his goodness like never before, if we want to see his goodness in our past, present, and future, we must start with a conversation that consists of talking, listening, and obeying. Proverbs 16:24 tells us, "Kind words are like honey—sweet to the soul and healthy for the body" (NLT). And Psalms 19:10-11 tells us the judgments of the Lord are "sweeter than honey and drippings of the honeycomb." There are no kinder words than the ones God speaks over us and to us. Engage in the goodness of conversation that drips like sweet honey over our lives.

Praying the Goodness of God

God, I thank you because you are good; good is who you are. And because you are good, you do good. I thank you that your goodness is stamped on all creation and holds this world together. Just when I feel as though the world, my world, is crashing down, I remember your great goodness and know you are holding it together.

You are the only absolute this life has to offer. Your goodness is an absolute to which I cling. Thank you for your Absolute Goodness—for sending your son, Jesus, to be the absolute example of your never-ending goodness.

Thank you for making me in your image. Thank you for instilling the gift of goodness in me so I can spread your goodness, your good news, to the ends of the earth. Holy Spirit, let the seed of goodness planted deep in my very being continually spring forth, extending to the broken and hurting world around me.

God, help my eyes, heart, and mind stay fixed on you as my standard of good—not to do and say what is good in my eyes, but to align my life to the holiness and righteousness of your great goodness.

Thank you that your goodness has gone before me and made the crooked places straight and made a way in the wilderness.

FOREVER IN MY *goodness*

Thank you for your goodness that follows me all the days of my life. Thank you for your goodness that is always pursuing me. Even when my life feels as though it has come to a screeching halt, thank you for your goodness that continually moves forward and floods the frozen moments.

Thank you for being in my past, present, and future. Holy Spirit, reveal your goodness in my past if I have missed it. I don't want to miss your goodness in a moment, so thank you for exposing your great goodness if I have overlooked it or was blinded by the trials of this life. Reveal any lies I may have believed about you and forgive me for believing or even entertaining the lies. Help me to see your goodness and replace the lies with the goodness of your truth.

Thank you for your goodness that guides me through this life. Without your Holy Spirit, your goodness, guiding and revealing, I would surely be lost in the wilderness forever. Let your goodness speak to my heart and mind as I walk this journey you have set my feet on. And as I lay down at night, I pray the goodness of your peace will calm my heart and mind and yet open my heart and mind to hear from you.

My heart and mind are set on your goodness, and I will see your goodness in the land of the living. I will no longer live just reciting, "You're good all the time"; forever on my lips and engraved on my heart and mind will be the declaration, "God, you are good all the time."

Chapter Ten Reflection

1. What kind of conversation do you typically have with God? Do you give a rundown of a list of things you want and/or need? Do you share your heart without giving pause to hear his voice? Or do you engage in a back-and-forth, real conversation?

2. Can you think of a time when you felt like you were in the wilderness? What did you hear? Did you hear the enemy, or were you tuned into God's voice?

3. Take a moment and write your own prayer of God's goodness, and then allow your heart and mind to hear his voice.

Epilogue

I MIRACULOUSLY DROVE THROUGH THE FLOOD that filled my eyes as the question "Where were you?" stood still in the space of my car, yet raced to heaven and responded back to my heart.

And suddenly, the picture of that haunting day froze in my mind. Though that summer day was warm and bright, in my mind, it was always dark and cold. Death by decapitation lingered over that day on the lake in a facade of victory that I chose to accept as reality. But the day when fear gripped me was now set free as I found my savior there.

I found myself once again, an innocent thirteen-year-old, holding that sweet baby boy. But this time, it was a bit different. I wasn't holding him by myself. Jesus, goodness, cradled my frail arms as I held the baby who had just lost the daddy he would never know. Jesus sat with me in a screened-in porch and ushered peace through my words to the curious minds of the children who were left in my care.

Jesus stayed with me in the pain of that day. God did not forsake anyone that day. The Holy Spirit wasn't quenched in the flood of death that day. In fact, they were there with each person who endured that tragic day.

For years, I doubted. For two weeks, I drove. And I asked one simple question. Then the darkest moment of my life was suddenly illuminated by the goodness of God. As soon as I surrendered, I was set free. I was free from the fear that gripped me. I was free from the doubt that the goodness of God went missing.

Fear lost its grip. Anxiety dried up and died. All because I allowed the goodness of God to be revealed in the worst day of my life. I haven't had a panic or anxiety attack since the day Jesus tore down the facade and replaced it with goodness.

God is present in every moment of our lives—our past, present, and future. His goodness is working in every moment of our lives. We just need to see it, embrace it, and let it bring freedom to our hearts and minds. His goodness is a sweet promise that sets us free to embrace the purpose he has for us.

Acknowledgments

Writing a book is truly a team effort. From the time God said, "Write," to the final production of the book, there was never a time I was alone in this process. To everyone who encouraged, believed, prayed, listened, and even helped with my boys, thank you.

To my husband, Brad—thank you for being my biggest fan. Your strong faith when I felt weak is what encouraged me to press on. You are a constant cheerleader, a trusted ear, and a faithful filter. Your continued belief that God would complete this work through me built my faith more than you will ever know.

To my precious boys, Jackson, Collin, and Harrison—I love you more than you could ever know. My prayer is that you saw the goodness and faithfulness of God as we walked this journey together. My heart's desire is for you to walk out your purpose faithfully as mighty men of God. Your many hugs, kisses, and words of encouragement filled my heart.

To my mom and dad—thank you for the consistent faith you have shown my entire life. You taught me that I could do anything but, more importantly, that I should do what God has asked me to do. You taught me to hear the voice of God and obey it faithfully, and for that I am eternally grateful. Thank you for your never-ending love. Love you always—your brown-eyed angel.

To my grandparents—thank you for blazing a path of faith for your families, for me. Mimi, your steadfast faith has forever marked my heart. Grandmother, your unending prayers have strengthened my faith. Granddaddy, your unconditional love is a true display of the Father's love. Granddaddy JD, you are missed more than we could ever show, but your legacy of faith lives on—thank you. My heart is forever grateful for the example each of you set, the prayers you prayed, and the love and legacy you have given.

Jennifer—you have talked with me and prayed for me in the darkest moments of my life. Your unwavering faith is an inspiration to everyone you meet and has touched my life more than you will ever know.

Lynsee—you are the iron to my iron. You are never short of making me a better friend, wife, mother, writer, or whatever hat we may be wearing. You are a constant encourager and faithful filter. Your sweet friendship is a constant refreshment to my soul. Thank you for praying and believing with me.

To my many faithful friends and Friendship Church—thank you to so many friends who have called, text, prayed, encouraged, and prophesied. I cherish each one you and am eternally blessed by your love and friendship.

Leafwood Publishers—thank you for seeing potential in me and for taking a chance on this girl pursuing the promises of God.

There is no greater thank you to be given than to Jesus, who walks with me daily; the Holy Spirit, who guides continually; and the Father, who loves endlessly. Thank you for weaving your beautiful goodness into my messy life. My heart forever proclaims your great goodness.

About the Author

Morgan is the wife of Brad Sugg and the mom of three amazing young men. Morgan and her family live in Frisco, Texas. She and Brad faithfully serve as the associate pastors at Friendship Church. She is the founder of Flourish Girl Night, writes regularly, and loves to speak to women.

Morgan is passionate about people experiencing the goodness of God, which sets them free and allows them to live out their God-given purpose. She believes every person was created on purpose for a purpose to impact the kingdom.

Morgan would love to connect with you online at
www.morgansugg.com

You can also join her on Instagram
@morgansugg

Or on Facebook at
www.facebook.com/MorganSuggWriter

www.ingramcontent.com/pod-product-compliance
Lightning Source LLC
Chambersburg PA
CBHW031112080526
44587CB00011B/948